MW00576239

VOM Books

The publishing division of

Serving persecuted Christians since 1967

vom.org

KARL MARX
AND THE
SATANIC ROOTS
OF COMMUNISM

RICHARD WURMBRAND

The Voice of the Martyrs

Karl Marx and the Satanic Roots of Communism
VOM Books
A division of The Voice of the Martyrs
1815 SE Bison Road
Bartlesville, OK 74006

Edited by Lynn Copeland

Interior design and layout by Genesis Group

Cover illustration by Scott Campbell

Printed in the United States of America

ISBN 978-0-88264-142-3

Library of Congress Catalog Card Number: 2021939568

Formerly published as *Marx and Satan* by Living Sacrifice Book Company (ISBN 978-0-89107-379-6)

Unless otherwise indicated, Scripture quotations are from the Holy Bible, English Standard Version. ESV® Text Edition: 2016. Copyright © 2001 by Crossway Bibles, a publishing ministry of Good News Publishers. Scripture quotations designated KJV are from the King James Version.

202107p007a1

CONTENTS

FOREWORD

When this book, titled *Marx & Satan*, was first published in 1986, Communist governments were persecuting and imprisoning Christians in the Soviet Union and in countries throughout Eastern Europe. Three years after this book was published, the Berlin Wall fell, and communism subsequently toppled in that region.

Following the end of the Cold War, some no longer viewed communism as a global threat. With China's participation in international trade, others believed its rapid economic growth would force the world's largest Communist country since 1949 to improve its poor human rights record, including the treatment of Christians.

But in truth, communism is not dead and its spreading global influence threatens and oppresses God's people today. As a government system, founded on the political ideology of Marxism, it is still being viewed as a viable solution to address the corruption and problems caused by capitalism.

After Richard Wurmbrand was ransomed out of Communist Romania where he was imprisoned for a total of fourteen years for his Christian witness, he was boldly outspoken about communism's effects on Christians and Christianity. He wrote:

> I cannot agree with what even well-known evangelists and mission directors are saying, that the principal foe today is the materialism of the West. *Today the principal enemy is Communism. Capitalism might have its evils, but it gives to the church the liberty to work at the salvation of souls. Communism...uproots religion.* The missionary energies must be concentrated upon the Communist lands.[1]

Although he wrote these words in 1969, at the peak of the Cold War and with the threat of Communist Cuba just ninety miles off Florida's coast, they are still relevant today. Communist governments oppress the church in China, Cuba, Vietnam, and Laos, while the ideology (Marxism) is influential in other nations such as Colombia, India, and Nepal. And in North Korea and the African country of Eritrea, dictators educated in Communist doctrine apply the ideology's values without a Communist political party.

In this book, Richard exposes the evils of the man behind both the political theory and the government system—Karl Marx—whose intent to abolish the church was not meant to be hidden, as Marx and Friedrich Engels wrote in the conclusion of

The Communist Manifesto: "The Communists disdain to conceal their views and aims."[2]

While Marx and Engels opened *The Communist Manifesto* by stating, "A spectre is haunting Europe—the spectre of communism,"[3] the "spectre" of communism has spread beyond Europe's borders throughout the world. By the end of the last century, experts estimate that communism is responsible for the deaths of roughly 100 million people worldwide.[4] However, there are no signs of such deaths slowing down.

Christians need to be aware of the true evil roots behind the man who founded communism. And more so as the "spectre" of communism, which inherently intends to "violently overthrow every social condition,"[5] is increasingly embraced by individuals in every nation around the globe today.

Richard Wurmbrand's findings on the following pages will also help readers to understand why the ideology and government system continue to persecute Christians and how ultimately communism cannot coexist with Christianity. "The Communist terror both inside and outside the countries they rule is the achievement of Marx's thoughts," wrote Richard. "There is no possibility of peaceful coexistence between Marxism and the Christian faith."[6]

—THE VOICE OF THE MARTYRS

INTRODUCTION

This work started as a small brochure containing only hints about possible connections between Marxism and Satanist beliefs.

No one had ventured to write about this before. Therefore I was cautious, even timid. But in the course of time more and more evidence has accumulated in my files, evidence I hope will convince you of the spiritual danger part and parcel of communism.

At the time of this writing, Marxism has governed over one-third of mankind. If it could be shown that the originators and perpetrators of this movement were indeed behind-closed-doors devil worshipers, consciously exploiting Satanic powers, would not such a startling realization require action?

If some were to reject my thesis out of hand, it would not surprise me. Science and technology advance at a rapid pace because we are always ready to scrap obsolescent machinery in favor of new conveniences. It is quite different in affairs of sociology or religion. Ideas die hard, and a mindset, unlike a computer chip, is not easily altered or replaced. Even fresh evidence may fail to persuade. The doors of some minds have rusty hinges. But I offer proofs to support my thesis, and I invite you to carefully consider them.

The Communists certainly took note of this book, which has been translated into Russian, Chinese, Romanian, German, Slovak, and other languages, and was smuggled into Iron Curtain countries in great quantities. For instance, the East Berlin journal *Deutsche Lehrerzeitung*, under the heading "The Killer of Marx," denounced my book vehemently, calling it "the most broadly based, provocative, and heinous work written against Marx."

Can Marx be so easily destroyed? Is this his Achilles' heel? Would Marxism be discredited if men knew about his connection with Satanism? Do enough people care?

Marxism is one of *the* great realities of modern life. Whatever your opinion of it, whether or not you believe in the existence of Satan, whatever importance you attach to the cult of Satan practiced in certain circles, I ask you to consider, weigh, and judge the documentation I present here.

I trust it will help you orient yourself to the problems with which Marxism still confronts every inhabitant of the globe today.

1

CHANGED LOYALTIES

Marx's Christian Writings

Today much of the world is still Marxist. Marxism in one form or another is embraced by many in capitalist countries, too. There are even Christians, and amazingly, clergymen, some in high standing, who are sure that while Jesus might have had the right answers about how to get to heaven, Marx had the right answers about how to help the hungry, destitute, and oppressed here on earth.

Marx, it is said, was deeply humane. He was dominated by one idea: how to help the exploited masses. What impoverishes them, he maintained, is capitalism. Once this rotten system is overthrown after a transitional period of dictatorship of the proletariat, a society will emerge in which everyone will work according to his abilities in factories and farms belonging to the collective, and will be rewarded according to his needs. There will be no state to rule over the individual, no wars, no revolution, only an everlasting, universal brotherhood.

In order for the masses to achieve happiness, more is needed than the overthrow of capitalism. Marx writes:

The abolition of religion as the illusory happiness of man is a requisite for their real happiness. The call to abandon their illusions about their conditions is a call to abandon a condition which requires illusions. The criticism of religion is, therefore, the criticism of this vale of tears of which religion is the halo.[1]

Allegedly, Marx was antireligious because religion obstructs the fulfillment of the Communist ideal, which he considered the only answer to the world's problems.

This is how Marxists explain their position, and sadly there are clergymen who explain it in the same way. Rev. Paul Oestreicher of Britain said in a sermon:

Communism, whatever its present varied forms of expression, both good and bad, is in origin a movement for the emancipation of man from exploitation by his fellowman. Sociologically, the Church was and largely still is on the side of the world's exploiters. Karl Marx, whose theories only thinly veil a passion for justice and brotherhood that has its roots in the Hebrew prophets, loathed religion because it was used as an instrument to perpetuate a status quo in which children were slaves and worked to death in order to make others rich here in Britain. It was no cheap jibe a hundred years ago to say that religion was the opium of the masses.... As members of the body of Christ we must come in simple penitence knowing that we owe a deep debt to every Communist.[2]

Marxism makes an impression on people's thinking because of its success, but success proves nothing. Witch doctors often succeed too. Success confirms error as well as truth. Conversely, failure can be constructive, opening the way to deeper truth. So an analysis of some of Marx's works should be made without regard to their success.

Who was Marx? In his early youth, Karl Marx professed to be and lived as a Christian. His first written work is called *The Union of the Faithful with Christ*. There we read these beautiful words:

Through love of Christ we turn our hearts at the same time toward our brethren who are inwardly bound to us and for whom He gave Himself in sacrifice.

Marx knew a way for men to become loving brethren toward one another—Christianity.

He continues:

Union with Christ could give an inner elevation, comfort in sorrow, calm trust, and a heart

susceptible to human love, to everything noble
and great, not for the sake of ambition and glory,
but only for the sake of Christ.[3]

At approximately the same time Marx writes in his thesis
Considerations of a Young Man on Choosing His Career:

Religion itself teaches us that the Ideal toward
which all strive sacrificed Himself for humanity, and who shall dare contradict such claims?
If we have chosen the position in which we can
accomplish the most for Him, then we can never
be crushed by burdens, because they are only
sacrifices made for the sake of all.[4]

Marx started out as a Christian believer. When he finished
high school, the following was written on his graduation certificate
under the heading "Religious Knowledge":

His knowledge of the Christian faith and morals is fairly clear and well grounded. He knows
also to some extent the history of the Christian
church.[5]

However, in a thesis written at the same time, he repeated six
times the word "destroy," which not even one of his colleagues used

in the exam. "Destroy" then became his nickname. It was natural for him to want to destroy because he spoke about mankind as "human trash" and said, "No man visits me and I like this, because present mankind may [an obscenity]. They are a bunch of rascals."

Marx's First Anti-God Writings

Shortly after Marx received this certificate, something mysterious happened in his life: he became profoundly and passionately anti-religious. A new Marx began to emerge.

He writes in a poem, "I wish to avenge myself against the One who rules above."[6] So he was convinced that there is One above who rules, but was quarreling with Him. Yet, the One above had done him no wrong. Marx belonged to a relatively well-to-do family. He had not faced hunger in his childhood. He was much better off than many fellow students. What produced such a terrible hatred for God? No personal motive is known. Was Karl Marx in this declaration only someone else's mouthpiece? We don't know.

At an age when most young men have beautiful dreams of doing good to others and preparing a career for themselves, the young Marx wrote the following lines in his poem "Invocation of One in Despair":

> So a god has snatched from me my all,
> In the curse and rack of destiny.
> All his worlds are gone beyond recall.
> Nothing but revenge is left to me.

I shall build my throne high overhead,
Cold, tremendous shall its summit be.
For its bulwark—superstitious dread.
For its marshal—blackest agony.

Who looks on it with a healthy eye,
Shall turn back, deathly pale and dumb,
Clutched by blind and chill mortality,
May his happiness prepare its tomb.[7]

Marx dreamt about ruining the world created by God. He said in another poem:

Then I will be able to walk triumphantly,
Like a god, through the ruins of their kingdom.
Every word of mine is fire and action.
My breast is equal to that of the Creator.[8]

The words "I shall build my throne high overhead" and the confession that from the one sitting on this throne will emanate only dread and agony remind us of Lucifer's proud boast: "I will ascend to heaven;…above the stars of God I will set my throne on high" (Isaiah 14:13).

Perhaps it was no coincidence that Mikhail Bakunin, who was for a time one of Marx's most intimate friends, wrote,

One has to worship Marx in order to be loved by him. One has at least to fear him in order to be tolerated by him. Marx is extremely proud, up to dirt and madness.[9]

The Satanist Church and *Oulanem*

Why did Marx wish such a throne?

The answer is found in a little-known drama which he also composed during his student years. It is called *Oulanem*. To explain this title, a digression is needed.

One of the rituals of the Satanist church is the black mass, which Satanist priests recite at midnight. Black candles are put in the candlesticks upside down. The priest is dressed in his ornate robes, but with the lining outside. He says all things prescribed in the prayer book, but reads from the end toward the beginning. The holy names of God, Jesus, and Mary are read inversely. A crucifix is fastened upside down or trampled upon. The body of a naked woman serves as an altar. A consecrated wafer stolen from a church is inscribed with the name Satan and is used for a mock Communion. During the black mass a Bible is burned. All those present promise to commit the seven deadly sins, as enumerated in Catholic catechisms, and never to do any good. An orgy follows.

Devil worship is very old. The Bible has much to say about—and against—it. For example, the Jews, though entrusted by God with the true religion, sometimes faltered in their faith and "sacrificed to demons" (Deuteronomy 32:17). And King Jeroboam of Israel once ordained priests "for the devils" (2 Chronicles 11:15, KJV).

So from time immemorial men have believed in the existence of the devil. Sin and wickedness are the hallmark of his kingdom, disintegration and destruction its inevitable result. The great concentrations of evil design in times past as well as in modern communism and Nazism would have been impossible without a guiding force, the devil himself. He has been the mastermind, the secret agent, supplying the unifying energy in his grand scheme to control mankind.

Characteristically, "Oulanem" is an inversion of a holy name. It is an anagram of Emmanuel, a biblical name of Jesus which means in Hebrew "God with us." Such inversions of names are considered effective in black magic.

We will be able to understand the drama *Oulanem* only in the light of a strange confession that Marx made in a poem called "The Player," later downplayed by both himself and his followers:

> The hellish vapors rise and fill the brain,
> Till I go mad and my heart is utterly changed.
> See this sword?
> The prince of darkness
> Sold it to me.
> For me he beats the time and gives the signs.
> Ever more boldly I play the dance of death.[10]

These lines take on special significance when we learn that in the rites of higher initiation in the Satanist cult an "enchanted" sword that ensures success is sold to the candidate. He pays for it by signing a covenant, with blood taken from his wrists, agreeing that his soul will belong to Satan after death.

(To enable the reader to grasp the horrid intent of these poems, I should mention—though with natural revulsion—that *The Satanic Bible*, after saying "the crucifix symbolizes pallid incompetence hanging on a tree," calls Satan "the ineffable Prince of Darkness who rules the earth."[11] As opposed to "the lasting foulness of Bethlehem," "the cursed Nazarene," "the impotent king," "fugitive and mute god," "vile and abhorred pretender to the majesty of Satan," the devil is called "the God of Light," with angels "cowering and trembling with fear and prostrating themselves before him" and "sending Christian minions staggering to their doom."[12])

Now I quote from the drama *Oulanem* itself:

> And they are also Oulanem, Oulanem.
> The name rings forth like death, rings forth
> Until it dies away in a wretched crawl.
> Stop, I've got it now! It rises from my soul
> As clear as air, as strong as my bones.[13]

> Yet I have power within my youthful arms
> To clench and crush you [i.e., personified
>   humanity] with tempestuous force,
> While for us both the abyss yawns in darkness.
> You will sink down and I shall follow laughing,
> Whispering in your ears, "Descend, come with
>   me, friend."[14]

The Bible, which Marx had studied in his high school years and which he knew quite well in his mature years, says that the devil will be bound by an angel and cast into the bottomless pit (*abyssos* in Greek; see Revelation 20:1–3). Marx desires to draw the whole of mankind into this pit reserved for the devil and his angels (Matthew 25:41).

Who speaks through Marx in this drama? Is it reasonable to expect a young student to entertain as his life's dream the vision of mankind entering into the abyss of darkness ("outer darkness" is a biblical expression for hell) and of himself laughing as he follows those he has led to unbelief? Nowhere in the world is this ideal cultivated except in the initiation rites of the Satanist church at its highest degrees.

When, in the drama, the time comes for Oulanem's death, his words are:

> Ruined, ruined. My time has clean run out.
> The clock has stopped, the pygmy house has
>   crumbled.
> Soon I shall embrace eternity to my breast, and
>   soon
> I shall howl gigantic curses on mankind.[15]

Marx had loved the words of Mephistopheles in *Faust:* "Everything in existence is worth being destroyed." *Everything,* including the proletariat and the comrades. Marx quotes these words in *The Eighteenth Brumaire of Louis Bonaparte*.[16] Stalin acted on them and destroyed even his own family.

Satan is called in *Faust* the spirit that denies everything. This is precisely Marx's attitude. He writes about "pitiless criticism of all that exists," "war against the situation in Germany," "merciless criticism of all." He adds, "It is the first duty of the press to undermine the foundations of the existing political system."[17] Marx said about himself that he is "the most outstanding hater of the so-called positive."[18]

The Satanist sect is not materialistic. It believes in eternal life. Oulanem, the person through whom Marx speaks, does not question this. He asserts eternal life, but as a life of hate magnified to its extreme.

It is worth noting that eternity for devils means torment. Note Jesus' reproach by demons: "Have you come here to torment us before the time?" (Matthew 8:29).

Marx is similarly obsessed:

> Ha! Eternity! She is our eternal grief,
> An indescribable and immeasurable Death,
> Vile artificiality conceived to scorn us,
> Ourselves being clockwork, blindly mechanical,
> Made to be the fool-calendars of Time and
>   Space,
> Having no purpose save to happen, to be
>   ruined,
> So that there shall be something to ruin.[19]

We begin now to understand what has happened to young
Marx. He had had Christian convictions, but had not led a
consistent life. His correspondence with his father testifies to his
squandering great sums of money on pleasures and his constant
quarreling with parental authority about this and other matters.
Then he seems to have fallen in with the tenets of the highly secret
Satanist church and received the rites of initiation.

Satan, who his worshipers see in their hallucinatory orgies,
actually speaks through them. Thus Marx is only Satan's mouthpiece when he utters in his poem "Invocation of One in Despair"
the words, "I wish to avenge myself against the One who rules
above."

Listen to the end of *Oulanem:*

> If there is a Something which devours,
> I'll leap within it, though I bring the world to
>   ruins—
> The world which bulks between me and the
>   abyss
> I will smash to pieces with my enduring curses.
>
> I'll throw my arms around its harsh reality,
> Embracing me, the world will dumbly pass
>   away,
> And then sink down to utter nothingness,
> Perished, with no existence—that would be
>   really living.[20]

Marx was probably inspired by the words of the Marquis de Sade:

> I abhor nature. I would like to split its planet, hinder its process, stop the circles of stars, overthrow the globes that float in space, destroy what serves nature, protect what harms it—in a word, I wish to insult it in my works.... Perhaps we will be able to attack the sun, deprive the universe of it, or use it to set the world on fire. These would be real crimes.

De Sade and Marx propagate the same ideas!

Honest men, as well as men inspired by God, often seek to serve their fellowmen by writing books to increase their store of knowledge, improve their morality, stimulate religious sentiments, or at least provide relaxation and amusement. The devil is the only being who consciously purveys only evil to humankind, and he does this through his servants.

As far as I know, Marx is the only renowned author who has ever called his own writings "s——t" [expletive deleted] and "swinish books."[21] He consciously, deliberately gives his readers filth. No wonder, then, that some of his disciples, Communists in Romania and Mozambique, forced prisoners to eat their own excrement and drink their own urine.[22]

In *Oulanem* Marx does what the devil does: he consigns the entire human race to damnation.

Oulanem is probably the only drama in the world in which all the characters are aware of their own corruption, and flaunt it and celebrate it with conviction. In this drama there is no black and white. There exist no Claudius and Ophelia, Iago and Desdemona. Here all are servants of darkness, all reveal aspects of Mephistopheles. All are Satanic, corrupt, doomed.

2

AGAINST ALL GODS

Satan in Marx's Family

When he wrote the works quoted in the last chapter, Marx, a premature genius, was only eighteen. His life's program had thus already been established. He had no vision of serving mankind, the proletariat, or socialism. He merely wished to bring the world to ruin, to build for himself a throne whose bulwark would be human fear.

At that point, correspondence between Karl Marx and his father included some especially cryptic passages. The son writes,

> A curtain had fallen. My holy of holies was rent
> asunder and new gods had to be installed.[1]

These words were written on November 10, 1837, by a young man who had professed Christianity until then. He had earlier declared that Christ was in his heart. Now this is no longer so. Who are the new gods installed in Christ's place?

The father replies,

> I refrained from insisting on an explanation about
> a very mysterious matter although it seemed
> highly dubious.[2]

What was this mysterious matter? No biographer of Marx has
explained these strange sentences.

On March 2, 1837, Marx's father writes to his son:

> Your advancement, the dear hope of seeing your
> name someday of great repute, and your earthly
> well-being are not the only desires of my heart.
> These are illusions I had had a long time, but I
> can assure you that their fulfillment would not
> have made me happy. Only if your heart remains
> pure and beats humanly and if *no demon* is able to
> alienate your heart from better feelings, only then
> will I be happy.[3]

What made a father suddenly express the fear of demonic
influence upon a young son who until then had been a confessed
Christian? Was it the poems he received as a present from his son
for his fifty-fifth birthday?

The following quotation is taken from Marx's poem "On
Hegel":

Words I teach all mixed up into a devilish muddle.
Thus, anyone may think just what he chooses to
think.[4]

Here also are words from another epigram on Hegel:

Because I discovered the highest,
And because I found the deepest through
    meditation,
I am great like a God;
I clothe myself in darkness like Him.[5]

In his poem "The Pale Maiden," he writes:

Thus heaven I've forfeited,
I know it full well.
My soul, once true to God,
Is chosen for hell.[6]

No commentary is needed.

Marx had started out with artistic ambitions. His poems and
drama are important in revealing the state of his heart; but having
no literary value, they received no recognition. Lack of success in
drama gave us a Goebbels, the propaganda minister of the Nazis;
in philosophy a Rosenberg, the purveyor of German racism; in
painting and architecture a Hitler.

Hitler was a poet too. It can be assumed that he never read Marx's poetry, but the resemblance is striking. In his poems Hitler mentions the same Satanist practices:

> On rough nights, I go sometimes
> To the oak of Wotan in the still garden,
> To make a pact with dark forces.
> The moonlight makes runes appear.
> Those that were sunbathed during the day
> Become small before the magic formula.[7]

"Wotan" is the chief god of German heathen mythology. "Runes" were symbols used for writing in olden times.

Hitler soon abandoned a poetic career, and so did Marx, who exchanged it for a revolutionary career in the name of Satan against a society that had not appreciated his poems. This is conceivably one of the motives for his total rebellion. Being despised as a Jew was perhaps another.

Two years after his father's expressed concern, in 1839, the young Marx wrote *The Difference Between Democritus' and Epicurus' Philosophy of Nature,* in the foreword to which he aligns himself with the declaration of Aeschylus, "I harbor hatred against all gods."[8] This he qualifies by stating that he is against all gods on earth and in heaven that do not recognize human self-consciousness as the supreme godhead.

Marx was an avowed enemy of all gods, a man who had bought his sword from the prince of darkness at the price of his soul. He had declared it his aim to draw all mankind into the abyss and to follow them laughing.

Could Marx really have bought his sword from Satan?

His daughter Eleanor says that Marx told her and her sisters many stories when they were children. The one she liked most was about a certain Hans Röckle.

> The telling of the story lasted months and months, because it was a long, long story and never finished. Hans Röckle was a witch…who had a shop with toys and many debts…. Though he was a witch, he was always in financial need. Therefore he had to sell against his will all his beautiful things, piece after piece, to the Devil…. Some of these adventures were horrifying and made your hair stand on end.[9]

Is it normal for a father to tell his little children horrifying stories about selling one's dearest treasures to the devil? Robert Payne in his book *Marx*[10] also recounts this incident in great detail, as told by Eleanor—how unhappy Röckle, the magician, sold the toys with reluctance, holding on to them until the last moment. But since he had made a pact with the devil, there was no escaping it.

Marx's biographer continues,

> There can be very little doubt that those intermi-
> nable stories were autobiographical. He had the
> Devil's view of the world, and the Devil's malig-
> nity. Sometimes he seemed to know that he was
> accomplishing works of evil.[11]

When Marx had finished *Oulanem* and other early poems in
which he wrote about having a pact with the devil, he had no
thought of socialism. He even fought against it. He was editor of
a German magazine, the *Rheinische Zeitung,* which "does not con-
cede even theoretical validity to Communist ideas in their present
form, let alone desire their practical realization, which it anyway
finds impossible.... Attempts by masses to carry out Communist
ideas can be answered by a cannon as soon as they have become
dangerous...."[12]

Marx Will Chase God from Heaven

After reaching this stage in his thinking, Marx met Moses Hess,
the man who played the most important role in his life, the man
who led him to embrace the Socialist ideal.

Hess calls him "Dr. Marx—my idol, who will give the last kick
to medieval religion and politics."[13] To give a kick to religion was
Marx's first aim, not socialism.

Georg Jung, another friend of Marx at that time, writes even
more clearly in 1841 that Marx will surely chase God from His
heaven and will even sue Him. Marx calls Christianity one of the
most immoral religions.[14] No wonder, for Marx now believed that

Christians of ancient times had slaughtered men and eaten their flesh.

These then were the expectations of those who initiated Marx into the depths of Satanism. There is no support for the view that Marx entertained lofty social ideals about helping mankind, saw religion as a hindrance in fulfilling this ideal, and for this reason embraced an antireligious attitude. On the contrary, Marx hated any notion of God or gods. He determined to be the man who would kick out God—all this before he had embraced socialism, which was only the bait to entice proletarians and intellectuals to embrace this devilish ideal.

Eventually Marx claims not to even admit the existence of a Creator. Incredibly, he maintained that mankind shaped itself. He wrote,

> Seeing that for the Socialist man all of so-called world history is nothing other than the creation of man through human work, than the development of nature for man, he has the incontestable proof of his being born from himself.... The criticism of religion ends with the teaching that man is the supreme being for man.

When no Creator is acknowledged, there is no one to give us commandments, or to whom we are accountable. Marx confirms this by stating, "Communists preach absolutely no morals." When the Soviets in their early years adopted the slogan, "Let us drive out the capitalists from earth and God from heaven," they were merely fulfilling the legacy of Karl Marx.

One of the peculiarities of black magic, as mentioned earlier, is the inversion of names. Inversions in general so permeated Marx's whole manner of thinking that he used them throughout. He answered Pierre-Joseph Proudhon's book *The Philosophy of Misery* with another book entitled *The Misery of Philosophy*. He also wrote, "We have to use instead of the weapon of criticism, the criticism of weapons."[15]

Here are further examples of Marx's use of inversion in his writing:

> Let us seek the enigma of the Jew not in his religion, but rather let us seek the enigma of his religion in the real Jew.[16]

> Luther broke the faith in authority, because he restored the authority of faith. He changed the priests into laymen, because he changed the laymen into priests.[17]

Marx used this technique in many places. He used what could be called typical Satanist style.

Shifting gears somewhat, men usually wore beards in Marx's time, but not beards like his, and they did not have long hair. Marx's manner and appearance were characteristic of the disciples of Joanna Southcott, a cultist priestess of an occult sect who claimed to be in contact with the ghost Shiloh.[18]

It is strange that some sixty years after her death in 1814,

> the Chatham group of Southcottians were joined
> by a soldier, James White, who, after his period
> of service in India, returned and took the lead
> locally, developing further the doctrines of Joanna
> …with a communistic tinge.[19]

Marx did not often speak publicly about metaphysics, but we can gather his views from the men with whom he associated. One of his partners in the First International (a federation of workers' groups) was Mikhail Bakunin, a Russian anarchist, who wrote:

> The Evil One is the satanic revolt against divine
> authority, revolt in which we see the fecund germ
> of all human emancipations, the revolution.
> Socialists recognise each other by the words "In
> the name of the one to whom a great wrong has
> been done."
>
>   Satan [is] the eternal rebel, the first free-
> thinker and the emancipator of worlds. He makes
> man ashamed of his bestial ignorance and obedi-
> ence; he emancipates him, stamps upon his brow
> the seal of liberty and humanity, in urging him to
> disobey and eat of the fruit of knowledge.[20]

Bakunin does more than praise Lucifer. He has a concrete program of revolution, but not one that would free the poor from exploitation. He writes:

> In this revolution we will have to awaken the Devil in the people, to stir up the basest passions. Our mission is to destroy, not to edify. The passion of destruction is a creative passion.[21]

Marx, along with Bakunin, formed the First International and endorsed this strange program. Marx and Engels said in *The Communist Manifesto* that the proletarian sees law, morality, and religion as "so many bourgeois prejudices, behind which lurk in ambush just as many bourgeois interests."

Bakunin reveals that Proudhon, another major Socialist thinker and at that time a friend of Karl Marx, also "worshiped Satan."[22] Hess had introduced Marx to Proudhon, who wore the same hairstyle typical of the nineteenth-century Satanist sect of Joanna Southcott.

Proudhon, in *The Philosophy of Misery*, declared that God was the prototype for injustice.

> We reach knowledge in spite of him, we reach society in spite of him. Every step forward is a victory in which we overcome the Divine.[23]

He exclaims,

> Come, Satan, slandered by the small and by
> kings. God is stupidity and cowardice; God is
> hypocrisy and falsehood; God is tyranny and
> poverty; God is evil. Where humanity bows be-
> fore an altar, humanity, the slave of kings and
> priests, will be condemned.... I swear, God, with
> my hand stretched out towards the heavens, that
> you are nothing more than the executioner of my
> reason, the sceptre of my conscience.... God is
> essentially anticivilized, antiliberal, antihuman.[24]

Proudhon declares God to be evil because man, His creation,
is evil. Such thoughts are not original; they are the usual content
of sermons delivered in Satanist worship.

Marx later quarreled with Proudhon and wrote a book to
refute his *Philosophy of Misery.* But Marx contradicted only minor
economic doctrines. He had no objection to Proudhon's demonic
anti-God rebellion.

Heinrich Heine, the renowned German poet, was a third intimate friend of Marx. He too was a Satan-fancier. He wrote:

> I called the devil and he came,
> His face with wonder I must scan;
> He is not ugly, he is not lame.
> He is a delightful, charming man.[25]

"Marx was a great admirer of Heinrich Heine…. Their relationship was warm, hearty."[26]

Why did he admire Heine? Perhaps for Satanist thoughts like the following:

> I have a desire…for a few beautiful trees before my door, and if dear God wishes to make me totally happy, he will give me the joy of seeing six or seven of my enemies hanged on these trees. With a compassionate heart I will forgive them after death all the wrong they have done to me during their life. Yes, we must forgive our enemies, but not before they are hanged.
>
> I am not revengeful. I would like to love my enemies. But I cannot love them before taking revenge upon them. Only then my heart opens for them. As long as one has not avenged himself, bitterness remains in the heart.

Would any decent man be an intimate friend of one who thinks like this?

But Marx and his entourage thought alike. Lunatcharski, a leading philosopher who was once minister of education of the USSR, wrote in *Socialism and Religion* that Marx set aside all contact with God and instead put Satan in front of marching proletarian columns.

It is essential at this point to state emphatically that Marx and his comrades, while anti-God, were not atheists, as present-day Marxists claim to be. That is, while they openly denounced and reviled God, *they hated a God in whom they believed.* They challenged not His existence, but His supremacy.

When the revolution broke out in Paris in 1871, creating a short-lived Paris Commune, the Communard Flourens declared, "Our enemy is God. Hatred of God is the beginning of wisdom."[27]

Marx greatly praised the Communards who openly proclaimed this aim. But what has this to do with a more equitable distribution of goods or with better social institutions? Such are only the outward trappings for concealing the real aim—the total eradication of God and His worship. We saw the evidence of this in such countries as Albania, and today in North Korea, where all churches, mosques, and pagodas have been closed.

Marx's Devilish Poetry

We see this clearly in Marx's poetry. In "Invocation of One in Despair" and "Human Pride," man's supreme supplication is for his own greatness. If man is doomed to perish through his own greatness, this will be a cosmic catastrophe, but he will die as a godlike being, mourned by demons. Marx's ballad "The Player" records the singer's complaints against a God who neither knows nor respects his art. This emerges from the dark abyss of hell, "bedeviling the mind and bewitching the heart, and his dance is the dance of death."[28] The minstrel draws his sword and throws it into the poet's soul.

Art emerging from the dark abyss of hell, bedeviling the mind—this reminds us of the words of the American revolutionary Jerry Rubin in *Do It:*

> We've combined youth, music, sex, drugs, and rebellion with treason—and that's a combination hard to beat.[29]

In his poem "Human Pride," Marx admits that his aim is not to improve the world or to reform or revolutionize it, but simply to ruin it and to enjoy its being ruined:

> With disdain I will throw my gauntlet
> Full in the face of the world,
> And see the collapse of this pygmy giant
> Whose fall will not stifle my ardour.
>
> Then will I wander godlike and victorious
> Through the ruins of the world
> And, giving my words an active force,
> I will feel equal to the Creator.[30]

Marx adopted Satanism after intense inner struggle. He ceased writing poems during a period of severe illness, a result of the tempest within his heart. He wrote at that time about his vexation at having to make an idol of a view he detested. He felt sick.[31]

The overriding reason for Marx's conversion to communism appears clearly in a letter of his friend Georg Jung to Arnold Ruge: it was not the emancipation of the proletariat, nor even the establishing of a better social order. Jung writes:

> If Marx, Bruno Bauer and Feuerbach associate to found a theological-political review, God would do well to surround himself with all his angels and indulge in self-pity, for these three will certainly drive him out of heaven.[32]

Were these poems the only expressly Satanist writings of Karl Marx? We do not know, because the bulk of his work is kept secret by those who guard his manuscripts.

In *The Revolted Man,* Albert Camus stated that thirty volumes of Marx and Engels have never been published and expressed the presumption that they are not much like what is generally known as Marxism. On reading this, I had one of my secretaries write to the Marx Institute in Moscow, asking if this assertion of the French writer is true.

I received a reply.

The vice director, one Professor M. Mtchedlov, after saying Camus lied, nevertheless confirmed his allegations. Mtchedlov wrote that of a total of one hundred volumes, only thirteen have appeared. He offered a ridiculous excuse for this: World War II forestalled the printing of the other volumes. The letter was written

in 1980, thirty-five years after the end of the war. And the State
Publishing House of the Soviet Union surely has sufficient funds.

From this letter it is clear that though the Soviet Communists
had all the manuscripts for one hundred volumes, they chose to
publish only thirteen. There is no other explanation than that most
of Marx's ideas were deliberately kept secret.

Marx's Ravaged Life

All active Satanists have ravaged personal lives, and this was the
case with Marx as well.

Arnold Künzli, in his book *Karl Marx: A Psychogram*,[33] writes
about Marx's life, including the suicide of two daughters and a
son-in-law. Three children died of malnutrition. His daughter
Laura, married to the Socialist Paul Lafargue, also buried three
of her children; then she and her husband committed suicide
together. Another daughter, Eleanor, decided with her husband to
do likewise. She died; he backed out at the last minute.

Marx felt no obligation to earn a living for his family, though
he could easily have done so through his tremendous knowledge
of languages. Instead, he lived by begging from Engels. He had
an illegitimate child by his maidservant, Helen Demuth. Later
he attributed the child to Engels, who accepted this comedy.
Marx drank heavily. David Rjazanov, director of the Marx-Engels
Institute in Moscow, admits this fact in his book *Karl Marx: Man,
Thinker and Revolutionist.*[34]

Eleanor was Marx's favorite daughter. He called her Tussy and
frequently said, "Tussy is me." She was shattered when she heard

about the scandal of illegitimacy from Engels on his deathbed. It was this that led to her suicide.

It should be noted that Marx, in *The Communist Manifesto,* had railed against capitalists "having the wives and daughters of their proletarians at their disposal." Such hypocrisy was not out of character for Karl Marx.

There was an even darker spot in the life of Marx, the great revolutionary. The German newspaper *Reichsruf* (January 9, 1960) published the fact that the Austrian chancellor Raabe donated to Nikita Khrushchev, then director of Soviet Russia, an original letter of Karl Marx. Khrushchev did not enjoy it, because it was proof that Marx had been a paid informer of the Austrian police, spying on revolutionaries.

The letter had been found accidentally in a secret archive. It indicated that Marx, as an informer, reported on his comrades during his exile in London. He received twenty-five dollars for each bit of information he turned up. His notes were about the revolutionary exiles in London, Paris, and Switzerland.

One of those against whom he informed was Ruge, who considered himself an intimate friend of Marx. Cordial letters between the two still exist.

Rolv Heuer describes Marx's ravaged financial life in *Genius and Riches:*

> While he was a student in Berlin, the son of papa Marx received 700 thalers a year pocket-money.[35]

This was an enormous sum because at that time only 5 percent of the population had an annual income greater than 300 thalers. During his lifetime, Marx received from Engels some six million French francs, according to the Marx Institute.

Yet he always lusted after inheritances. While an uncle of his was in agony, Marx wrote to Engels, "If the dog dies, I would be out of mischief."[36] To which Engels answers, "I congratulate you for the sickness of the hinderer of an inheritance, and I hope that the catastrophe will happen now."[37]

"The dog" died, and Marx wrote on March 8, 1855,

> A very happy event. Yesterday we were told about the death of the ninety-year-old uncle of my wife. My wife will receive some one hundred Lst; even more if the old dog has not left a part of his money to the lady who administered his house.[38]

He did not have any kinder feelings for those who were much nearer to him than his uncle. He was not even on speaking terms with his mother. In December 1863 he wrote to Engels,

> Two hours ago a telegram arrived to say that my mother is dead. Fate needed to take one member of the family. I already had one foot in the grave. Under the circumstances I am needed more than the old woman. I have to go to Trier about their inheritance.[39]

This was all he had to say at his mother's passing.

In addition, the relationship between Marx and his wife was demonstrably poor. She abandoned him twice but returned each time. When she died, he did not even attend her funeral.

Always in need of funds, Marx lost much money at the stock exchange, where he, the great economist, knew only how to lose.

Marx was an intellectual of high caliber, as was Engels. But their correspondence is full of obscenities, unusual for their class of society. Foul language abounds, and there is not one letter in which one hears an idealist speaking about his humanist or Socialist dream.

Since the Satanist sect is highly secret, we have only reports about the possibilities of Marx's connections with it. But his disorderly life is undoubtedly another link in the chain of evidence already considered.

3

RUINED FAITH

Engels's Counter-Conversion

Since Friedrich Engels figures prominently in Marx's life, I will give brief material about him. Engels had been brought up in a pietistic family. In fact, in his youth he had composed beautiful Christian poems. After meeting Marx, he wrote about him:

> Who is chasing wild endeavor? A black man from
> Trier [Marx's birthplace], a remarkable monster.
> He does not walk or run, he jumps on his heels
> and rages full of anger as if he would like to catch
> the wide tent of the sky and throw it to the earth.
> He stretches his arms far away in the air; the
> wicked fist is clenched, he rages without ceasing,
> as if ten thousand devils had caught him by the
> hair.[1]

Engels had begun to doubt the Christian faith after reading a book written by a liberal theologian, Bruno Bauer. He had had a great struggle in his heart. He wrote at that time,

> I pray every day, indeed almost all day, for truth,
> and I have done so ever since I began to doubt,
> but still I cannot go back. My tears are welling as
> I write.[2]

Engels never found his way back to the Word of God, joining instead the one whom he himself had called "the monster possessed by ten thousand devils."[3] He had experienced a counter-conversion.

What kind of person was Bruno Bauer, the liberal theologian who played a decisive role in the destruction of Engels's Christian faith and who endorsed Marx in his new anti-Christian ways? Did he have any connection with demons?

Like Engels himself, Bauer started life as a believer and later as a conservative theologian, even writing against critics of the Bible. Afterward he himself became a radical critic of the holy Scriptures and creator of a materialistic Christianity which insisted that Jesus was only human, not the Son of God. Bauer wrote to his friend Arnold Ruge, also a friend of Marx and Engels, on December 6, 1841:

> I deliver lectures here at the university before a
> large audience. I don't recognize myself when I
> pronounce my blasphemies from the pulpit. They

are so great that these children, whom nobody should offend, have their hair standing on end. While delivering the blasphemies, I remember how I work piously at home writing an apology of the holy Scriptures and of the Revelation. In any case, it is a very bad demon that possesses me as often as I ascend the pulpit, and I am so weak that I am compelled to yield to him…. My spirit of blasphemy will be satisfied only if I am authorized to preach openly as professor of the atheistic system.[4]

The man who convinced him to become a Communist was the same Moses Hess who had previously convinced Marx. Hess wrote, after meeting Engels in Cologne,

He parted from me as an overzealous Communist.
This is how I produce ravages.[5]

To produce ravages—was this Hess's supreme purpose in life? It is Lucifer's, too.

The traces of having been a Christian never disappeared from Engels's mind. In 1865, he expressed his admiration for the song of the Reformation, "A Mighty Fortress Is Our God," calling it "a triumphal hymn which became the Marseillaise of the sixteenth century."[6] There are also other such pro-Christian statements from his pen.

The tragedy of Engels is moving, and even more gripping than that of Marx. Here is a wonderful Christian poem written in his youth by the man who would later become Marx's greatest accomplice in the attempted destruction of religion:

> Lord Jesus Christ, God's only son,
> O step down from Thy heavenly throne
> And save my soul for me.
> Come down in all Thy blessedness.
> Light of Thy Father's holiness,
> Grant that I may choose Thee.
> Lovely, splendid, without sorrow is the joy
>   with which we raise,
> Saviour, unto Thee our praise.
>
> And when I draw my dying breath
> And must endure the pangs of death,
> Firm to Thee may I hold;
> That when my eyes with dark are filled
> And when my beating heart is stilled,
> In Thee shall I grow cold.
> Up in Heaven shall my spirit praise
>   Thy name eternally,
> Since it lies safe in Thee.
>
> O were the time of joy but nigh
> When from Thy loving bosom I

Might draw new life that warms.
And then, O God, with thanks to Thee,
Shall I embrace those dear to me
Forever in my arms.
Ever, ever, ever-living,
    Thee abiding to behold
Shall my life anew unfold.

Thou earnest Humankind to free
From death and ill, that there might be
Blessings and fortune everywhere.
And now with this, Thy new descent,
On Earth all shall be different;
To each man shalt Thou give his share.[7]

After Bruno Bauer had sown doubts in his soul, Engels wrote
to some friends,

It is written, "Ask and it shall be given unto you."
I seek truth wherever I have the hope of finding
at least a shadow of it. Still I cannot recognize
your truth as the eternal truth. Yet it is written,
"Seek and ye shall find. Who is the man among
you who would give to his child a stone, when it
asks for bread? Even less will your Father who is
in heaven."

Tears come into my eyes while I write this. I am moved through and through, but I feel I will not be lost. I will come to God, after whom my whole soul longs. This, too, is a witness of the Holy Spirit. With this I live and with this I die.

…The Spirit of God witnesses to me, that I am a child of God.[8]

Engels was very well aware of the danger of Satanism. In his book *Schelling, Philosopher in Christ,* Engels wrote:

Since the terrible French Revolution, an entirely new, devilish spirit has entered into a great part of mankind, and godlessness lifts its daring head in such an unashamed and subtle manner that you would think the prophecies of Scripture are fulfilled now. Let us see first what the Scriptures say about the godlessness of the last times.

The Lord Jesus says in Matthew 24:11–14: "Many false prophets shall rise, and shall deceive many. And because iniquity shall abound, the love of many shall wax cold. But he that shall endure unto the end, the same shall be saved. And this gospel of the kingdom shall be preached in all the world for a witness unto all nations; and then shall the end come." And then in verse 24: "There shall arise false Christs, and false prophets, and shall show great signs and wonders; insomuch that, if it were possible, they shall deceive the very elect." And St. Paul says, in II Thessalonians 2:3ff.: "That man of sin shall be revealed, the son of perdition, who opposes and exalts himself above all that is God, or that is worshipped…. [The coming of the Wicked] is after the working of Satan with all power and signs and lying wonders, and with all deceivableness of unrighteousness in them that perish; because they received not the love of the truth, that they might be saved. *And for this cause God shall send them strong delusion, that they should believe a lie:* that they all might be damned who believed not the truth, but had pleasure in unrighteousness."[9]

Engels quotes Scripture after Scripture, just as the most Bible-believing theologian would do.

He continues:

We have nothing to do any more with indifference or coldness toward the Lord. No, it is an open, declared enmity, and in the place of all sects and parties we have now only two: Christians and anti-Christians…. We see the false prophets among us…. They travel throughout Germany and wish to intrude everywhere; they teach their

Satanic teachings in the market-places and bear
the flag of the Devil from one town to another,
seducing the poor youth, in order to throw them
in the deepest abyss of hell and death.[10]

He finishes this book with the words of Revelation:

"Behold, I come soon. Keep what you have,
that nobody takes away from you your crown."
Amen![11]

The man who wrote such poems and such warnings against
Satanism, the man who prayed with tears to beware of this danger,
the man who recognized Marx as being possessed with a thousand
devils, became Marx's closest collaborator in the devilish fight, "for
Communism abolishes eternal truths, it abolishes all religion, and
all morality."[12]

Liberal theology had accomplished this monstrous change.
Thus it shares with Marx and Engels the guilt for the tens of millions of innocents killed by communism to date. What spiritual
tragedy!

Marx Hates Whole Nations

Shifting now from Engels to Marx, Marx's whole attitude and
conversation were Satanic in nature.

Though a Jew, he wrote a pernicious anti-Jewish book called *The Jewish Question.* In 1856, he wrote in *The New York Tribune* an article entitled "The Russian Loan," in which we read:

> We know that behind every tyrant stands a Jew, as a Jesuit stands behind every Pope. As the army of the Jesuits kills every free thought, so the desire of the oppressed would have chances of success, the usefulness of wars incited by capitalists would cease, if it were not for the Jews who steal the treasures of mankind. It is no wonder that 1856 years ago Jesus chased the usurers from the Jerusalem temple. They were like the contemporary usurers who stand behind tyrants and tyrannies. The majority of them are Jewish. The fact that the Jews have become so strong as to endanger the life of the world causes us to disclose their organization, their purpose, that its stench might awaken the workers of the world to fight and eliminate such a canker.

Did Hitler say anything worse than this?

(Strangely, Marx also wrote to the contrary, in *The Capital,* Volume I, under the heading "The Capitalist Character of Manufacture": "In the front of the chosen people it was written that they are the property of Jehovah.")

Many other Jewish Communists imitated Marx in their hatred of Jews. Ruth Fisher, renowned German Jewish Communist leader and a member of Parliament, said, "Squash the Jewish capitalists, hang them from the lamp posts; tread them under your feet."[13] Why just the Jewish capitalists and not the others remains an unanswered question.

Marx hated not only the Jews, but also the Germans: "Beating is the only means of resurrecting the Germans." He spoke about "the stupid German people…the disgusting national narrowness of the Germans" and said that "Germans, Chinese, and Jews have to be compared with peddlers and small merchants."[14] He called the Russians "cabbage-eaters."[15] The Slavic peoples were "ethnic trash."[16] He expressed his hatred of many nations, but never his love.

Marx wrote in his new year's roundup of 1848 about "the Slavic riffraff," which included Russians, Czechs, and Croats. These "retrograde" races had nothing left for them by fate except "the immediate task of perishing in the revolutionary world storm." "The coming world war will cause not only reactionary classes and dynasties, but entire reactionary peoples, to disappear from the face of the earth. And that will be progress." "Their very name will vanish."[17]

Neither Marx nor Engels were concerned about the destruction of millions of people. The former wrote,

> A silent, unavoidable revolution is taking place
> in society, a revolution that cares as little about

the human lives it destroys as an earthquake cares
about the houses it ravages. Classes and races that
are too weak to dominate the new conditions of
existence will be defeated.

In contrast, Hitler, who desired only the enslavement and not
the destruction of these nations, was much more humane than
Marx.

Engels wrote in the same vein:

The next world war will make whole reactionary
peoples disappear from the face of the earth. This,
too, is progress.[18]

Obviously this cannot be fulfilled without crush-
ing some delicate national flower. But without
violence and without pitilessness nothing can be
obtained in history.[19]

Marx, the man who posed as a fighter for the proletariat, called
this class of people "stupid boys, rogues, asses."

Engels well knew what to expect from them. He wrote, "The
democratic, red, yes, even the Communist mob, will never love
us."

Marx identified black people with "idiots" and constantly
used the offensive term "n——r" [racial epithet deleted] in private
correspondence.

He called his rival Ferdinand Lassalle "the Jewish n——r" [racial epithet deleted] and made it very clear that this was not intended as an epithet of disdain for just one person.

> It is now absolutely clear to me that, as both the shape of his head and his hair texture shows, he is descended from the Negroes who joined Moses' flight from Egypt (unless his mother or grandmother on the paternal side hybridized with a n——r).... The pushiness of the fellow is also n——r-like [racial epithets deleted].

Marx even championed slavery in North America. For this, he quarreled with his friend Proudhon, who had advocated the emancipation of slaves in the United States. Marx wrote in response,

> Without slavery, North America, the most progressive of countries, would be transformed into a patriarchal country. Wipe North America from the map of the world and you will have anarchy—the complete decay of modern commerce and civilization. Abolish slavery and you will have wiped America off the map of nations.[20]

Marx also wrote, "The Devil take the British!"[21]

In spite of such denunciations, there are plenty of British, as well as American, Marxists.

Satan Is in the Family

Marx's favorite daughter, Eleanor, with her father's approval, married Edward Eveling. He lectured on such subjects as "The Wickedness of God." (Just as Satanists do. Unlike atheists, they do not deny the existence of God, except to deceive others; they know of His existence, but describe Him as wicked.) In his lectures he tried to prove that God is "an encourager of polygamy and an instigator to theft." He advocated the right to blaspheme.[22] The following poem describes the attitudes of his movement toward Satanism:

> To thee my verses, unbridled and daring,
> Shall mount, O Satan, king of the banquet.
> Away with thy sprinkling, O priest, and thy
> droning.
> For never shall Satan, O priest, stand behind
> thee.

> Thy breath, O Satan, my verses inspire,
> When from my bosom the gods I defy.
> Of kings pontifical, of kings inhuman:
> Thine is the lightning that sets minds to shaking.

> O soul that wanderest far from the straight way,
> Satan is merciful. See Heloisa!
> Like the whirlwind spreading its wings,

He passes, O people, Satan the great!
Hail, of reason the great Vindicator!
Sacred to thee shall rise incense and vows!
Thou hast the god of the priest disenthroned.[23]

4

TOO LATE

A Housemaid's Revelation

An American, Commander Sergius Riis, had been a disciple of Marx. Grieved by the news of his death, he went to London to visit the house in which the admired teacher had lived. The family had moved. The only one whom he could find to interview was Marx's former housemaid Helen Demuth. She said these amazing words about him:

> He was a God-fearing man. When very sick, he prayed alone in his room before a row of lighted candles, tying a sort of tape measure around his forehead.[1]

This suggests phylacteries, implements worn by Orthodox Jews during their morning prayers. But Marx had been baptized in the Christian religion, had never practiced Judaism, and later became a fighter against God. He wrote books against religion and brought up all his children as atheists. What was this ceremony that an ignorant maid considered an occasion of prayer? Jews, saying their prayers with phylacteries on their foreheads, don't usually have a row of candles before them. Could this have been some kind of magic practice?

We also know that Marx, a presumed atheist, had a bust of Zeus in his study. In Greek mythology Zeus, a cruel heathen deity, transformed himself into a beast and took Europe captive—as did Marxism later.

Family Letters

Another possible hint is contained in a letter written to Marx by his son Edgar on March 31, 1854. It begins with the startling words, "My dear devil."[2] Who has ever known of a son addressing his father like this? But that is how a Satanist writes to his beloved one. Could the son have been initiated as well?

Equally significant, Marx's wife addresses him as follows, in a letter of August 1844:

> Your last pastoral letter, high priest and bishop of
> souls, has again given quiet rest and peace to your
> poor sheep.[3]

Marx had expressed, in *The Communist Manifesto,* his desire to abolish all religion, which one might assume would include abolishing the Satanist cult too. Yet his wife refers to him as high priest and bishop. Of what religion? The only European religion with high priests is the Satanist one. What pastoral letters did he, a man believed to have been an atheist, write? Where are they? This is a part of Marx's life that has remained unresearched.

Biographers' Testimonies

Some biographers of Marx have undoubtedly had a suspicion about the connection between devil-worship and the subject of their book. But not having the necessary spiritual preparation, they could not understand the facts they had before their eyes. Still, their testimony is interesting.

The Marxist Franz Mehring wrote in his book *Karl Marx:*

> Although Karl Marx's father died a few days after his son's twentieth birthday, *he seems to have observed with secret apprehension the demon in his favorite son.*[4]

> Henry Marx did not think and could not have thought that the rich store of bourgeois culture which he handed on to his son Karl as a valuable heritage for life *would only help to deliver the demon he feared.*[5]

Marx died in despair, as all Satanists do. On May 20, 1882, he wrote to Engels, "How pointless and empty is life, but how desirable!"[6]

Marx was a contemporary of great Christians: the composer Mendelssohn, the philanthropist Dr. Barnardo, the preachers

Charles Spurgeon and General William Booth. All lived near him in London. Yet he never mentions them. They went unobserved.

There is a secret behind Marx that few Marxists know about. Lenin wrote, "After half a century, not one of the Marxists has comprehended Marx."[7]

The Secret Behind Lenin's Life

There was a secret behind Lenin's life too.

When I wrote the first edition of the present book, I knew of no personal involvement of Lenin with any rituals of the Satanist sect. Since then, I have read *The Young Lenin* by Leon Trotsky, who was Lenin's intimate friend and coworker. He writes that Lenin, at the age of sixteen, tore the cross from his neck, spat on it, and trod it underfoot, a very common Satanist ceremony.

There is not the slightest doubt that Lenin was dominated by Satanist ideology. How else could one explain the following quotation from his letter to the Russian writer Maxim Gorki, dated November 13–14, 1913:

> Millions of sins, mischiefs, oppressions, and physical epidemics, are more easily discovered by the people, and therefore less dangerous, than the thinnest idea of a spiritual little god, even if disguised in the most decorous garb.[8]

In the end Satan deceived him, as he does all his followers. Lenin was moved to write as follows about the Soviet state:

> The state does not function as we desired. How
> does it function? The car does not obey. A man
> is at the wheel and seems to lead it, but the car
> does not drive in the desired direction. It moves
> as another force wishes.[9]

What is this other mysterious force that supersedes even the
plans of the Bolshevik leaders? Did they sell out to a force that they
hoped to master, but that proved more powerful than even they
anticipated and drove them to despair?

In a letter of 1921, Lenin wrote:

> I hope we will be hanged on a stinking rope. And
> I did not lose the hope that this would happen,
> because we cannot condemn dirty bureaucracy. If
> this happens, it will be well done.[10]

This was Lenin's last hope after a whole life of struggle for the
Communist cause: to be justly hanged on a stinking rope. This
hope was not fulfilled for him, but almost all of his coworkers
were eventually executed by Stalin after confessing publicly that
they had served other powers than the proletariat they pretended
to help.

What a confession from Lenin: "I hope we will be hanged on
a stinking rope."

It is interesting to note that at the age of thirteen, Lenin wrote
what could be called prophetic poetry foretelling the bankruptcy

in which his life would end. He had decided to serve mankind, but without God. These were his words:

> Sacrificing your life freely for others,
> It is a pity you will have the sad fate
> That your sacrifice will be completely fruitless.[11]

What a contrast to the words of another fighter, the apostle Paul, who wrote toward the end of his life:

> I have fought the good fight, I have finished the race.... Henceforth there is laid up for me the crown of righteousness, which the Lord, the righteous judge, will award to me on that day. (2 Timothy 4:7,8)

There exists a "too late" in our spiritual affairs. Esau repented with many tears for having sold his birthright, but the deal could not be undone. And Lenin, founder of the Soviet state, said on his deathbed,

> I committed a great error. My nightmare is to have the feeling that I'm lost in an ocean of blood from the innumerable victims. It is too late to return. To save our country, Russia, we would have needed men like Francis of Assisi. With ten men like him we would have saved Russia.

5

A CRUEL COUNTERFEIT

Bukharin, Stalin, Mao, Ceausescu, Andropov

It might be instructive at this point to take a look at some modern Marxists. Bukharin, secretary general of the Communist International and one of the chief Marxist doctrinaires in the twentieth century, as early as the age of twelve, after reading the book of Revelation in the Bible, longed to become the Antichrist. Realizing from Scripture that the Antichrist had to be the son of the apocalyptic great whore, he insisted that his mother confess to having been a harlot.

About Stalin he wrote, "He is not a man, but a devil."[1]

Too late Bukharin realized into whose hands he had fallen. In a letter that he made his wife memorize just before his arrest and execution, he said,

> I am leaving life. I am lowering my head.... I feel
> my helplessness before a hellish machine.[2]

He had helped erect a guillotine—the Soviet state—that had killed millions, only to learn in the end that its design had been made in hell. He had desired to be the Antichrist. He became instead a victim of the Enemy.

Similarly, Kaganovitch, Stalin's brother-in-law and closest collaborator, writes about him in his diary:

> I started to understand how Stalin managed to make himself a god. He did not have a single human characteristic.... Even when he exhibited some emotions, they all did not seem to belong to him. They were as false as the scale on top of armor. And behind this scale was Stalin himself— a piece of steel. For some reason I was convinced that he would live forever.... He was not human at all....
>
> Rosa [his wife] says he makes her climb a tree wearing nothing but stockings. I have a feeling he is not human at all. He is too unusual to be a regular human being. Although he looks like an ordinary man. Such a puzzle. What is it I'm writing? Am I raving mad, too?

Stalin described to Kaganovitch his spiritual exercise. Believers of various religions engage in the practice of meditation on what is beautiful, wise, and good, to help them become more loving. Stalin indulged in just the opposite practice.

He told Kaganovitch:

> When I have to say good-bye to someone, I
> picture this person on all fours and he becomes
> disgusting. Sometimes I feel attached to a per-
> son who should be removed for the good of
> the cause. What do you think I do? I imagine
> this person s——g [expletive deleted], exhaling
> stench, farting, vomiting—and I don't feel sorry
> for this person. The sooner he stops stinking on
> this earth, the better. And I cross this person out
> of my heart.

One of Stalin's amusements was to put green glasses on the
eyes of horses to make them see hay as grass. Even worse, he put
dark glasses of atheism on the eyes of men to keep them from
seeing God's pastures, reserved for believing souls.

The diary contains many revealing insights:

> Many times Stalin spoke of religion as our
> most vicious enemy. He hates religion for many
> reasons, and I share his feelings. Religion is a cun-
> ning and dangerous enemy.... Stalin also thinks
> that separation from children should be the main
> punishment for all parents belonging to sects, ir-
> respective of whether they were convicted or not.

I think he secretly engaged in astrology. One peculiar feature of his always astonished me. He always talked with some veiled respect about God and religion. At first, I thought I was imagining it, but gradually I realized it was true. But he was always careful when the subject came up. And I was never able to find out exactly what his point of view was. One thing became very clear to me—his treatment of God and religion was very special. For example, he never said directly there was no God....

People ceased somehow to be their own selves in his presence. They all admired him and worshiped him. I don't think he enjoyed any great love of the nation: he was above it. It may sound strange, but he occupied a position previously reserved only for God.

Part and parcel of the tragedy of human existence is the fact that one has enemies and is sometimes obliged to fight them. Marx took delight in this sad necessity. His favorite saying, which he often repeated, was, "There is nothing more beautiful in the world than to bite one's enemies."[3]

No wonder his follower Stalin said that the greatest joy is to cultivate a person's friendship until he lays his head confidently on your bosom, then to implant a dagger in his back—a pleasure not to be surpassed.[4]

Marx had expressed the same idea long before. He wrote to Engels about comrades with whom he disagreed:

> We must make these rogues believe that we continue our relationship with them, until we have the power to sweep them away from our road, in one manner or another.[5]

It is significant that many of Stalin's comrades-in-arms spoke about him as demonic.

Milovan Djilas, prominent Communist leader of Yugoslavia who was personally well acquainted with Stalin, wrote:

> Was it not so that the demonic power and energy of Stalin consisted in this, that he made the [Communist] movement and every person in it pass to a state of confusion and stupefaction, thus creating and ensuring his reign of fear…?[6]

He also says about the whole ruling class of the USSR:

> They make a semblance of believing in the ideal of socialism, in a future society without classes. In reality, they believe in nothing except organized power.[7]

Even Stalin's daughter, Svetlana Alliluyeva, who never learned about the depths of Satanism, wrote,

> Beria [the Soviet minister of interior affairs] seems to have had a diabolic link with all our family.... Beria was a frightening, wicked demon.... A terrible demon had taken possession of my father's soul.[8]

Svetlana further mentions that Stalin considered goodness and forgiving love to be worse than the greatest crime.[9]

Such is the Satanic priesthood that rules almost half of mankind and which orders terrorist acts all over the world.

Stalin was the illegitimate child of a landlord by a servant-maid. His father, fearing notoriety, bribed a cobbler to marry the pregnant girl, but the affair became known. During his childhood Stalin was mocked as a bastard. During Stalin's teen years, his real father was found murdered. Stalin was suspected, but no proof could be found against him.

Later, as a seminary student, he joined Communist circles. There he fell in love with a girl named Galina. Since the Communists were poor, Galina was given the assignment to become the mistress of a rich man and so provide the Party with money. When Stalin himself voted for this proposal, she cut her veins.

Stalin himself committed robberies for the Party, and in this he was very successful. He appropriated none of the stolen money for himself.

He was also assigned the duty of infiltrating the Czarist police. He had to play a dual role, denouncing secondary Party members in order to find out police secrets and protect more important Communists.

As a young man, therefore, Stalin had the worst possible heredity, education, and development. Thus he was easily susceptible to Satanist influence. He became what his name, Stalin, means: a man of steel, without the slightest human emotion or pity.

(Andropov, late premier of the Soviets, produced the same impression as Stalin. The French minister of external affairs, Claude Cheysson, who met him, described Andropov in *Le Monde* as "a man without warmth of soul, who works like a computer.... He shows no emotions.... He is extremely dispassionate.... He is accurate in words and gestures like a computer.")

Stalin, like Marx, Engels, and Bauer before him, started out as a believer. At fifteen, he wrote his first poem, which begins with the words, "Great is the Almighty's providence." He became a seminarian because he felt it his calling.[10] There he became first a Darwinist, then a Marxist.

When he began to write as a revolutionary, the first pseudonyms he used were "Demonoshvili,"[11] meaning something like "the demoniac" in the Georgian language, and "Besoshvili,"[12] "the devilish."

Other evidences of Satanist persuasion among Marxist leaders are also significant. Troitskaia, daughter of the Soviet marshal Tuhatchevsky, one of the top men of the Red Army who was later shot by Stalin, wrote of her father that he had a picture of Satan in the east corner of his bedroom, where the Orthodox usually put their icons.

When a certain Communist in Czechoslovakia was named head of the State Council for Religious Affairs, an institution whose purpose is to spy on believers and persecute them, he took the name "Hruza," which means in Slovak "horror," an appellation used for "devil."

One of the leaders of a terrorist organization in Argentina took upon himself the nickname "Satanovsky."

Anatole France, a renowned French Communist writer, introduced some of the greatest intellectuals of France to communism. At an exhibition of demoniac art in Paris, one of the pieces shown was the specific chair used by that Communist writer for presiding over Satanist rituals. Its horned armrests and legs were covered with goat's fur.[13]

Britain's center of Satanism is Highgate Cemetery in London, where Karl Marx is buried. Mysterious rites of black magic are celebrated at this tomb.[14] It was the place of inspiration for the Highgate Vampire, who attacked several girls in 1970.[15] Hua Kuo-Feng, director of Red China, also paid it his respects.

Ulrike Meinhof, Eselin, and other German Red terrorists have also been involved in the occult.[16]

One of the oldest devil-worshiping sects, the Syrian Yezidi, was written up in a Soviet atheistic magazine, *Nauka I Religia* (July 1979). It is the *only* religious sect about which the magazine wrote not one word of criticism.

Furthermore, Mao Tse-tung wrote:

> From the age of eight I hated Confucius. In our
> village there was a Confucianist temple. With all
> my heart, I wished only one thing: to destroy it to
> its very foundations.[17]

Is it normal for an eight-year-old child to wish only the destruction of his own religion? Such thoughts belong to demonic characters.

At the other extreme is St. Paul of the Cross, who since his youth spent three hours in prayer every night.

Cult of Violence

Engels wrote in *Anti-Dubring,* "Universal love for men is an absurdity." And in a letter to a friend he said, "We need hate rather than love—at least for now."

Che Guevara learned his Marxist lessons well. In his writings he echoes Engels's sentiments:

> Hate is an element of fight—pitiless hate against
> the foe, hate that lifts the revolutionist above the
> natural limitation of man and makes him become
> an efficient, destructive, cool, calculating, and
> cold killing machine.

This is what the devil wishes to make of men. He has succeeded all too well with many notorious leaders of the human race.

In our lifetime we have witnessed more than our share: Hitler, Eichmann, Mengele, Stalin, Mao, Andropov, Pol Pot.

Marx writes in *The Communist Manifesto*,

> The Communists despise making a secret of their opinions and intentions. They openly declare that their aims can be reached only through the violent overthrow of the whole existing social structure.

Further:

> There is only one method to shorten the murderous pains of death of the old society, the bloody birth pangs of the new society; only one method to simplify and concentrate them, that is revolutionary terrorism.[18]

There have been many revolutions in history. Each had an objective. The American Revolution, for example, was fought for national independence, the French Revolution for democracy. Marx is the only one who formulates as his aim a "permanent revolution," terrorism and bloodshed for revolution's sake. There is no purpose to be attained; violence to the point of paroxysm is its only objective. This is what distinguishes Satanism from ordinary human sinfulness.

Marx called terrorists executed for murder in Czarist Russia "immortal martyrs" or "amazingly capable fellows."[19]

Engels wrote, too, of the "bloody revenge we take." This expression occurs often. "In the interior [of Russia], what a splendid development. The attempts at murder become frequent." "Leaving aside the problem of morality...for a revolutionist any means are right which lead to the purpose, the violent, as the seemingly tame."[20]

The Marxist Lenin, while living under the democratic rule of Kerensky in Russia, said,

> What is needed is wild energy and again energy. I wonder, yea more, I am horrified that more than half a year has passed in speaking about bombs and not one single bomb has been fabricated.[21]

A further insight into the fundamental attitudes of Communists can be gained from a few brief quotes.

> Marx: "We make war against all prevailing ideas of religion, of the state, of country, of patriotism. The idea of God is the keynote of a perverted civilization. It must be destroyed."
>
> Lenin: "We have to use any ruse, dodge, trick, cunning, unlawful method, concealment, and veiling of the truth. The basic rule is to exploit the conflicting interests of the capitalist states."

Lenin: "Atheism is an integral part of Marxism. Marxism is materialism. We must combat religion. This is the ABC of all materialism and consequently of Marxism."

Lenin, in an address in 1922: "First we shall take Eastern Europe, then the masses of Asia. After that, we shall surround and undermine the U.S.A., which will fall into our hands without a struggle—like an overripe fruit."

Khrushchev: "If anyone believes our smiles involve abandonment of the teachings of Marx, Engels and Lenin, he deceives himself. Those who wait for that must wait until a shrimp learns to whistle."

Satanist Cruelty

Solzhenitsyn reveals in his monumental *Gulag Archipelago*[22] that the hobby of Yagoda, the Soviet Union's minister of interior affairs, was to undress and, naked, shoot at images of Jesus and the saints. A couple of comrades joined him in this. Another Satanist ritual practiced in Communist high places!

Why should men allegedly representing the proletariat shoot at the image of Jesus, a proletarian, or the virgin Mary, a poor woman?

Some Pentecostal Christians recall an incident that took place in Russia during World War II. One of their preachers had exorcised a devil who threatened, upon leaving the possessed, "I will take revenge." Several years later the Pentecostal preacher who had performed the exorcism was shot for his faith. The officer who executed him said just before pulling the trigger, "Now we are even."

Are Communist officers sometimes possessed by devils? Do they perhaps serve as Satan's instruments of revenge against Christians who seek to overthrow his throne? There is no doubt.

In Russia, in Stalin's day, some Communists killed a number of innocents in the cellars of the police. After their bloody deed, one of the henchmen had second thoughts and went from corpse to corpse, apologizing: "I did not intend to do this. I don't know you. Speak to me, move, forgive me." One of his comrades then killed him. A third was converted and later related the incident.

Russkaia Misl, a Russian-language magazine in France, reported (March 13, 1975) the following from the Soviet Union:

D. Profirevitch, in Russia, had a daughter and a son whom he brought up in the faith. Naturally, they had to attend Communist schools. At the age of twelve the daughter came home and told her parents, "Religion is a capitalist superstition. We are living in new times." She dropped Christianity altogether. Afterward she joined the Communist Party and became a member of the Secret Police. This was a terrible blow to her parents.

Later the mother was arrested. Under Communist rule no one possesses anything, whether it be children, a wife, or personal liberty. The state can take them away at any time.

After the mother's arrest, the son exhibited great sorrow. A year later he hanged himself. D. Profirevitch found this suicide letter:

> Father, will you judge me? I am a member of the
> Communist youth organization. I had to sign that
> I would report everything to the Soviet authori-
> ties. One day the police called me, and Varia, my

sister, asked me to sign a denunciation against
Mother because as a Christian she is considered
a counterrevolutionist. I signed. I am guilty of
her imprisonment. Now they have ordered me to
spy on you. The consequence will be the same.
Forgive me, Father; I have decided to die.

The suicide of the son was followed by the jailing of the
father.[23]

Priest Zynoviy Kovalyk was arrested by the Bolsheviks in 1941
and was confined in the Brygidka jail in Lviv, Ukraine. When the
Germans put the Bolsheviks to flight that same year, the people of
the city found the priest's blood-stained body nailed to the wall by
the arms and legs, as if it were the crucified Lord. They also found
about six thousand massacred prisoners, shot in the nape of the
neck, whom the Bolsheviks had piled on top of each other in the
cellars and covered over with plaster.

Dr. O. Sas-Yavorsky (from the United States), after the capture
of Lviv by the Germans near the end of June 1941, went search-
ing for his imprisoned father and saw in the jail a priest nailed
to a cross. Into his slashed stomach the Communists had placed
the body of an unborn baby, taken from the womb of its mother,
whose corpse lay on the blood-soaked floor. Other eyewitnesses
recognized that this was the body of the renowned missionary
Father Kovalyk.[24]

Generally, to the Communists human life is cheap. Lenin
wrote during the civil war,

> It would be a shame not to shoot men for not
> obeying the draft and avoiding mobilization.
> Report more often about the results.[25]

During the Spanish Civil War, Communists killed four thousand Catholic priests.

A renowned Russian Orthodox priest named Dudko reported that six Communists entered the house of Father Nicholas Tchardjov, pulled out his hair, gouged out his eyes, made many cuts on his body, passed a pressing iron over it, then shot him with two bullets. This happened on the Eve of St. Nicholas. It was not only a crime against the priest, but also a mockery of the saint.

The Western press reported on March 10, 1983, that in Zimbabwe three thousand of the Ndebele tribe were killed by the soldiers of the Communist dictator Mugabe. The army had been trained by North Korean instructors. Tribe members were asked to shoot their grown-up sons themselves; if they refused, they were shot along with their sons.

The devil apes God by promising still waters and green pastures which are not his to give. Therefore he must pretend. And the less he can offer, the more he must pretend. To gain a foothold, he puts on a false front (did you ever wonder about Communist front organizations?) and makes benevolent gestures. But he delivers only misery, death, and destruction—"awful, complete, universal, and pitiless."

The devil is jealous and becomes enraged at spiritual beauty. It offends him. Since he cannot be beautiful—he lost his primal beauty because of his pride—he does not want anyone else to be. If it were not for the saints' spiritual beauty, the devil would not seem so ugly. Therefore he wishes to deface all beauty.

This is why Christians in the Romanian Communist prison of Piteshti, as well as other Communist jails, were tortured—not only to betray the secrets of the underground church, but to blaspheme.

Regimes under which such horrors occur again and again, regimes that turn even Christians into murderers and denouncers of innocent victims, can only be abhorred by the children of God. Whoever bids them Godspeed is a partaker in their evil deeds (2 John 11).

Satanic Sin

I have written that Marxism is Satanic. But is not every sin Satanic by its very nature?

I pondered long about this. Then I had a dream one night that clarified my thinking.

In my dream I saw a prostitute hooking young men who were just leaving church. I asked her, "Why did you choose this particular place to work?"

She replied, "My delight is to lead young men into sin just as they come from worship. The Greek word for worship in the New Testament is *proskyneō,* which means etymologically 'to kiss.' The worshiper stepping out of the house of prayer still has the imprint of Jesus' kisses on his mouth. What a satisfaction to defile him just then, to make him wallow in the bed of lasciviousness and then say to him, 'You see, Jesus to whom you prayed could not keep you from sin for even five minutes. He is not your Savior. My master is more powerful than He.'"

Sexual impurity is a common human sin. Mephistopheles asks Faust to seduce Gretchen just as she is walking to church with a prayer book in her hand. This is Satanic.

To write, read, or view pornography is another common sin. But it is a characteristic of American pornography, which promotes incest, pederasty, and perversion, that it is full of the names of God, Christ, and Mary. With every obscenity there is a sacred word, with every ugly gesture a heavenly expression, to defile and profane the holy. This is Satanic.

To slay the innocent is a very common sin as well. To crucify Jesus, the Son of God, between two thieves in order to suggest guilt by association is Satanic.

To kill political enemies, to make war and stir up revolution—even with mass killings—proves human sinfulness. But the Russian Communists, having killed millions of their enemies, turned their violence against even their friends, including their most illustrious comrades, the chief perpetrators of their revolution. This is the seal of Satanism. It is revolution not for attaining a goal, but revolution and killing for killing's sake, what Marx called "the permanent revolution."

Of twenty-nine members and candidates in the Central Committee of the Soviet Communists in 1917, the year of the revolution, only four had the good fortune to depart this life before being deprived of it. One of the four was posthumously declared "an enemy of the revolution." Thirteen were sentenced to death by their own comrades or disappeared. Two were so persecuted by Stalin that they committed suicide.[26]

To be a criminal or a Mafioso is a heinous human sin, but the Satanic goes beyond even what the Mafia allows.

Tomasso Buscetta, a representative of the Sicilian Mafia, who became a police informer and revealed the crimes of that organization, said:

> Crime is a necessity that one cannot avoid, but that always has a reason. With us gratuitous crime, which is an end in itself or the result of an individual impulse, is excluded. We exclude, for example, "transversal vendetta," i.e., the calculated killing of someone near the target of our crime, such as a wife, children, or relatives.

Satanic crime is of another order. Hitler killed millions of Jews, including babies, with the excuse that Jews had done harm to the German people. For the Communists it was a matter of course to imprison and torture the family members of a person they considered guilty. When I was jailed, it was taken for granted that my wife must be jailed too, and that my son must be excluded from all schooling.

Marxism is not an ordinary sinful human ideology. It is Satanic in its manner of sinning, as it is Satanic in the teachings it purveys. Only in certain circumstances has it openly avowed its Satanic character.

One can judge a teacher by his disciples. The painter Picasso said, "An artist must discover the way to convince his public of the full truth of his lies."[27]

Who was the man who wrote this monstrosity? The same who wrote, "I came to communism as one comes to a fountain.... My adherence to communism is the logical consequence of my entire life and work."[28]

So one becomes a Marxist because his ideal is a lie. How sad!

To gain an insight into the life and thinking of a Satanist, one need only read a few mild excerpts from the writing of Aleister Crowley (1875–1947), notorious for his involvement in occult practices:

> Pity not the fallen. I never knew them. I console not. I hate the consoler and the consoled.[29]

> The wolf betrays only the greedy and treacherous, the raven betrays only the melancholy and dishonest. But I am he of whom it is written: He shall deceive the very elect....
>
> I have feasted myself on the blood of the saints, but I am not suspected of men to be their enemy, for my fleece is white and warm, for my teeth are not the teeth of one that tears flesh, and my eyes are mild, and they know me not as the chief of the lying spirits.[30]

Beautiful art thou, O Babylon, and desirable….
O Babylon, Babylon, thou mighty mother, that
ride upon the crowned beasts, let me be drunken
upon the wine of your fornication; let your kisses
wanton me unto death.[31]

Crowley quotes a multitude of sayings like this from complete-ly unknown older Satanist works, unavailable to the uninitiated.

Blasphemous Versions of the Lord's Prayer

The Soviet newspaper *Sovietskaia Molodioj*, February 14, 1976, added a new and shattering proof of the connections between Marxism and Satanism. It described how militant Communists stormed churches and mocked God under the Czarist regime. For this purpose the Communists used a blasphemous version of the "Our Father":

Our Father, which art in Petersburg,
Cursed be your name,
May your Kingdom crumble,
May your will not be fulfilled, yea, not even in
    hell.
Give us our bread which you stole from us,
And pay our debts, as we paid yours until now.
And don't lead us further into temptation,
But deliver us from evil—the police of Plehve
    [the Czarist prime minister],

And put an end to his cursed government.
But as you are weak and poor in spirit and in
     power and in authority,
Down with you for all eternity. Amen.[32]

The ultimate aim of communism in conquering new countries is not to establish another social or economic system. *It is to mock God and praise Satan.*

The German Socialist Student Union also published a parody of the Lord's Prayer, indicating that the "true" meaning of the prayer upholds capitalism:

Our Capital, which art in the West,
May your investments be sure,
May you make a profit.
May your shares increase in value,
On Wall Street as in Europe.
Our daily sale give us today, and extend our
     credits,
As we extend those of our debtors.
And do not lead us into bankruptcy,
But deliver us from the trade unions,
For thine is half the world and the power, and
     the riches, for 200 years.
                    Mammon.[33]

The identification of Christianity with the interests of capitalism is outrageous. The true church knows that capitalism, too, is stained with blood, for every economic system bears the marks of sin. Christians oppose communism not from the viewpoint of capitalism, but of the kingdom of God, which is their true social ideal. The above is nothing less than Satanic mockery of Jesus' most holy prayer, as is the one published by the Soviets.

Mockery of the Lord's Prayer is customary in many Communist lands. Ethiopian children were taught to pray as follows:

> Our Party which rulest in the Soviet Union,
> Hallowed be thy name,
> Thy Kingdom come,
> Thy will be done in Ethiopia and in the whole
>   world.
> Give us this day our daily bread,
>   and don't forgive the trespasses of the
>   Imperialists as we will not forgive them.
> And may we resist the temptation to abandon
>   the fight,
> And deliver us from the evils of Capitalism.
>   Amen.

Over an Ethiopian Lutheran radio station confiscated by the Communist government, a Satanist version of the Bible was broadcast. First Corinthians 13 sounded like this:

> Though I speak all the languages and have no enmity toward the landlords and capitalists, I have become as sounding brass.... Class hatred suffers no exploitation and is brutal. Class hatred envies their riches and vaunts itself with the successful revolutions in many Socialist states.... And now abide faith, hope, and class hatred, but the greatest of these is revolutionist hatred.

During the general strike organized by the French Communists in 1974, workers were called to march in the streets of Paris shouting the slogan, *"Giscard d'Estaing est foutu, les démons sont dans la rue!* (Giscard d'Estaing [then French president] is done with. Demons are now in the street!)"[34] Why not "the proletariat" or "the people"? Why this evocation of Satanic forces? What has this to do with the legitimate demands of the working class to have better salaries?

Deification of Communist Leaders

Communist leaders have been and are deified. Listen to the following poem honoring Stalin in *Pravda* (Moscow, March 10, 1939). (*Pravda* was the central organ of the Communist Party in the USSR.)

> The sun shines mildly and who would not know
>   that you are this sun?

The pleasant noise of the sea waves sings an ode
    to Stalin.
The blinding snowy peaks of mountains sing the
    praise of Stalin.
The millions of flowers and meadows thank you.
Likewise the covered tables.
The beehives thank you.
The fathers of all young heroes thank you,
    Stalin;
Oh, Lenin's heir, you are for us Lenin himself.

Thousands of such poems have been composed. Here is
another hymn to Stalin of extraordinary fervor and beauty,
reminding one of Eastern Byzantine Christianity in the fourth and
following centuries:

O great Stalin, O leader of the peoples,
Thou who broughtest man to birth,
Thou who purifiest the earth,
Thou who restorest the centuries,
Thou who makes bloom the Spring,
Thou who makes vibrate the musical chords.

Thou, splendor of my Spring, O Thou
Sun reflected from millions of hearts.

The foregoing hymn was published in *Pravda* in August 1936. In May 1935, the same official Party newspaper had published the following extraordinary effusion:

> He commands the sun of the enemies to set.
> He spoke, and the East for friends became a
> > great glow.
> Should he say that coal turns white,
> It will be as Stalin wills....
> The master of the entire world—remember—is
> > now Stalin.

A much later composition by a leading Soviet poet shows development in style but hardly in subject matter:

> I would have compared him to a white
> > mountain—but the mountain has a
> > summit.
> I would have compared him to the depths of the
> > sea—but the sea has a bottom.
> I would have compared him to the shining
> > moon—but the moon shines at midnight,
> > not at noon.
> I would have compared him to the brilliant
> > sun—but the sun radiates at noon, not at
> > midnight.

Mao Tse-tung has been hailed as the one "whose mind created the world." Kim Il-sung, dictator of North Korea, was also deified, as was Nicolae Ceausescu, Communist dictator of Romania.

Ceausescu was another Stalinist figure. He was the object of a personality cult and was likened to Julius Caesar, Alexander the Great, Pericles, Cromwell, Napoleon, Peter the Great, and Abraham. This distinguished roster, it seems, is not enough. So he was also called "our lay God."

(By the way, post-Communist Romania, which did not allow international religious conventions, permitted a witches' convention in the spring of 1979 in Curtea-de-Argesh.)

In Bucharest there was a museum containing gifts brought by the people to Ceausescu. In it was a watercolor painted by a blind man who regained his sight through a miracle. He attributed it to the fact that "he concentrated all his thoughts on the President, who not only can make the blind to see but can move the Carpathian mountains."

Another portrayal showed Ceausescu with King Vlad Tsepesh, who was known as "the vampire Dracula" because he used to impale his adversaries. In similar fashion, Stalin magnified the personality of Czar Ivan the Terrible.

The administrators of Romania today were Communist Party members. The leopard has not changed its spots.

6

A SPIRITUAL
WARFARE

The Little and the Big Devils

According to current official Marxist doctrine, which, as has been illustrated, is only a disguise, neither God nor the devil exists. Both are fancies. Because of this teaching, Christians are persecuted by the Communists.

However, the Soviet newspaper *Kommunisma Uzvara*[1] (April 1974) reported that many atheist circles were created in Red Latvia's schools. The name given the children in the fourth through sixth grades was "little devils," while seventh graders were called "servants of the devil." In another school eighth graders had the name "faithful children of the devil." At a meeting the children came clothed as devils, complete with horns and tails.

Thus, it was forbidden to worship God, though devil worship was openly permitted and even encouraged among children of school age. This was the hidden objective of the Communists when they seized power in Russia.

In Vitebsk (USSR), Zoia Titova, a member of the Communist youth organization, was caught practicing black magic. When her case was brought before the assembly of Communist youth, there was unanimous refusal to punish her, though members who decided to worship God were expelled. The Communists consider it wrong to believe in God. For this "crime," many children were separated from their families and kept in special atheist boarding schools.

Incredibly, the Communists even wanted to make Satan-worshipers of church leaders. A Russian Orthodox priest named Platonov, an anti-Jewish agitator, went over to the side of the Communists when they came to power in Russia. For this, he was made a bishop and became a Judas who denounced members of his flock to the Secret Police, well knowing they would be severely persecuted.

One day, while on a bus, he met his sister Alexandra, an abbess who had been arrested many times, apparently with her brother's knowledge. He asked her, "Why don't you speak to me? Don't you recognize your brother?" She answered, "You ask why? Father and Mother would turn over in their graves. You are serving Satan." Though an official Orthodox bishop in the Soviet Union, he replied, "Perhaps I am Satan myself."[2]

Pravoslavnaia Rus writes,

> The Orthodox cathedral in Odessa, so much
> loved by the Odessites, became the meeting place
> of Satanists soon after the Communists came

to power.... They gathered also in Slobodka-
Romano and in Count Tolstoi's former home. [3]

Then follows a detailed account of Satanist masses said by
deacon Serghei Mihailov, of the treacherous Living Church, an
Orthodox branch established in connivance with the Communists.
An attendant describes the Satanist mass as a "parody of the
Christian liturgy, in which human blood is used for Communion."
These masses took place in the cathedral before its main altar.

Also in Odessa, a statue of Satan used to be exhibited in the
Museum of the Atheists. It was called Bafomet. At night, Satanists
would gather in the museum for prayer and chanting before the
statue.

Religious Obscenities

It might be in some sense "logical" that Communists would arrest
priests and pastors as counterrevolutionaries. But why were priests
compelled by the Marxists in the Romanian prison of Piteshti to
say Mass over excrement and urine? Why were Christians tortured
into taking Communion with these as the elements? Why such an
obscene mockery of religion? Why did the Romanian Orthodox
priest Roman Braga, whom I knew personally when he was a prisoner of the Communists, and who moved to the United States,
have his teeth knocked out one by one with an iron rod in order to
make him blaspheme?

The Communists had explained to him and others, "If we kill
you Christians, you go to heaven. But we don't want you to be
crowned martyrs. You should curse God first and then go to hell."

In the prison of Piteshti the Communists would force a very religious prisoner to be "baptized" daily by putting his head into the barrel in which his fellow-sufferers had fulfilled their necessities, meanwhile obliging the other prisoners to sing the baptismal service.

A theology student was forced to dress in white sheets (in imitation of Christ's robe), and a phallus made out of soap was hung around his neck with a string. Christians were beaten to insanity to force them to kneel before such a mocking image of Christ. After they had kissed the soap, they had to recite part of the liturgy.[4]

Some prisoners were compelled to take off their trousers and sit with their naked bottoms on open Bibles.[5]

Such blasphemous practices were perpetrated for at least two years with the full knowledge of the Party's top leadership. What have such indignities to do with socialism and the well-being of the proletariat? Were their anticapitalist slogans not merely pretexts for organizing Satanic blasphemies and orgies?

Marxists are supposed to be atheists who believe in neither heaven nor hell. In these extreme circumstances, Marxism has lifted its atheistic mask to reveal its true face, the face of Satanism. Communist persecution of religion might have a human explanation, but the fury of such perverse persecution can only be Satanic.

In Romanian prisons and in the Soviet Union as well, nuns who would not deny their faith were raped anally, and Baptist girls had oral sex forced on them.[6]

Many prisoners who were so treated died as martyrs, but the Communists were not satisfied with this. Using Luciferian techniques, they made martyrs die blaspheming because of the delirium provoked by torture.

Only once in all his works did Marx ever write about torture. During his own lifetime, many of his followers were tortured by Russian Czarist authorities. Since Marx is usually described as a humanist, one would expect him to write with horror about such an abominable practice. But his only comment was,

> Torture alone has given rise to the most ingenious mechanical inventions and employed many honorable craftsmen in the production of the instruments.[7]

Torture is productive; it leads to ingenious inventions—this is all Marx had to say about the subject. No wonder Marxist governments have surpassed all others in torturing their opponents! This alone displays the Satanic nature of Marxism.

Marxism also is based on a hatred for God. In 1923, in the Soviet Union, mock trials of God were held in the presence of Trotsky and Lunatcharski.[8] But such opposition to God and His people do not belong only to the past.

Satanist desecrations of Catholic churches occurred in the 1970s in Upyna, Dotnuva, Zanaiciu, Kalvarija, Sede, etc.—localities in Lithuania. One about which we know happened in Alsedeai on September 22, 1980.[9]

In his book *Psychiatric Hospital 14, Moscow,* Georgi Fedotov tells of his conversation with the psychiatrist Dr. Vladimir Levitski about a Christian named Argentov who was detained there. The physician says, "You are pulling your friend Eduard toward God and we toward the Devil. So I'm using my rights as a psychiatrist to deny you and your friends access to him."

The Christian Salu Daka Ndebele was interrogated by the Secret Police of Maputo in Communist Mozambique. The officer said to him, "We want to kill your God." He raised his gun toward the head of the prisoner and declared, "This is my God. With this I have the power of life and death. If your God comes here, I will shoot Him dead myself."[10]

In Chiasso, Communist Angola, Communists slaughtered animals in a church and placed their heads on the altar and pulpit. A poster proclaimed, "These are the gods whom you adore." Pastor Aurelio Chicanha Saunge was killed, together with one hundred and fifty parishioners.[11]

When the Catholic Lithuanian priest Eugene Vosikevic was killed, his mouth was found to have been filled with bread, an apparent Satanist ritual.[12]

Vetchernaia Moskva, a Communist newspaper, let pass a Freudian slip of the pen:

> We do not fight against believers and not even against clergymen. We fight against God to snatch believers from Him.[13]

A "fight against God to snatch believers from Him" is the only logical explanation for the Communist fight against religion.

We do not wonder at these words in a Soviet newspaper. Marx had said it already in his book *German Ideology.* Calling God "the absolute Spirit," as his teacher Hegel had done, he wrote, "We are concerned with a highly interesting question: the decomposition of the Absolute Spirit."

It was not a fight against false belief in a nonexistent God that preoccupied him. He believed that God does exist and wanted to see this Absolute Spirit decompose, like many prisoners of the Communists who were made to rot in jail.

In Albania a priest, Stephen Kurti, was sentenced to death for having baptized one child. Baptisms must be performed in secret in many Communist lands, including North Korea.

The prosecutor at the trial of Metropolitan Benjamin of Leningrad said,

> The whole Orthodox church is a subversive orga-
> nization. Properly speaking, the entire church
> ought to be in prison.

The only reason all Christians were not in jail in the former Soviet Union was that the Communists were not quite powerful enough. But the will to destroy is there. Unrestrained by the Spirit of God and empowered by the forces of evil, they would indeed destroy the whole earth, including themselves.

In the former Soviet Union baptisms could be officiated only after registration. Persons wishing to be baptized or to have their child baptized presented their identity cards to the representative of the church board, who in turn reported them to the state authorities. The result was persecution. Kolkhozniks (workers on collective farms) had no identity cards and could therefore baptize their children only secretly.[14] Many Protestant pastors received prison sentences for baptizing people.

The Communist fight against baptism presupposes belief in its value for a soul. Religious people in Israel or Pakistan or Nepal oppose baptism in the name of their own religious outlook, because it is a Christian seal. But for atheists—as Communists clearly declare themselves to be—baptism should mean nothing. Supposedly it neither benefits nor harms the baptized. Why then do these Communists fight against baptism? It is because Communists "fight against God to snatch believers from Him." Their ideology is not really inspired by atheism, but by a fervent hatred for God.

"Among other purposes," said Lenin, "we created our party specifically for the fight against any religious deceiving of the people."

Occult Practices

More about the relationship between Marxism and the occult can be found in *Psychic Discoveries Behind the Iron Curtain*[15] by Sheila Ostrander and Lynn Schroder. It is highly significant that the Communist East had been much more advanced than the West in research about the dark forces manipulated by Satan.

Dr. Eduard Naumov, a member of the International Association of Parapsychologists, was arrested in Moscow. The Moscow physicist L. Regelsohn, a Hebrew-Christian who took his defense, tells us the reason for his arrest: Naumov endeavored to keep the psychic sphere of life free from the domination of evil forces that used parapsychology as a new weapon for the oppression of the human soul.[16]

In Czechoslovakia, Bulgaria, etc., the Communist Party spent huge sums on secret investigation into this science. They hid from the West information about what happened in the twenty parapsychological institutes located in the Soviet Union.

Komsomolskaia Pravda (Moscow) published a lengthy article about hypnotists who help people "regress to past lives." For the induction process they use the following suggestions:

> You descend into earth, deeper, even deeper. You and the earth become one.... You are deep in the earth. You are surrounded by thick darkness.... Around you is eternal night....
>
> Now we approach a spot of light far away... nearer and nearer. We sneak through a small hole to the sky, leaving our own body deep in the earth.... We overcome the frontiers of time... and we return to your past.

In such articles the Soviets used intentional double-talk. Aware that some might become frightened, they were purposefully reserved, claiming they only inform without agreeing. But what would readers think of an editor who reprinted provocative articles and lustful pictures endlessly from *Playboy* while claiming that he did not agree fully with what he was purveying to the public?

Soviet writers said clearly that this "time machine" was not science fiction. "Transpersonalism" offered this voyage in time.

As noted, in the Satanist black masses, all prayers are said from the end to the beginning, and the priestly robe is worn inside out. Inversion is the Satanist rule, and this is applied even to the doctrine of reincarnation. Whereas Indian devotees are concerned about their future reincarnations and try to better themselves by obeying what they believe to be God's commandments, the Satanists offer a return to former incarnations. They care nothing about a better future in eternity.

Marxism as a Church

Just as Satan came to Jesus with Bible verses, so Marx used texts of Scripture, though with much distortion.

Volume 2 of *The Works of Marx and Engels* opens with Jesus' words to His disciples (John 6:63), as quoted by Marx in his book *The Holy Family:* "It is the spirit which gives life." Then we read:

> Criticism [his criticism of all that exists] so loved the masses that it sent its only-begotten son [i.e., Marx], that whosoever believes in him should not perish but have a life of criticism. Criticism became masses and lived among us, and we saw its glory as the glory of the only-begotten Son of the Father. Criticism did not consider it

> robbery to be equal with God, but made itself of
> no reputation, taking the form of a bookbinder,
> and humbled itself up to nonsense—yes, critical
> nonsense in foreign languages.[17]

Those knowledgeable in Scripture will recognize this as a parody of biblical verses (John 3:16; 1:14; Philippians 2:6–8). Here again, Marx declares his own works to be "nonsense," as well as "swinish books."

Marxism is a religion, and it even "uses" Scripture. Its main work, *The Capital* by Marx, is called "the Bible of the working class." Marx considered himself "the Pope of Communism."[18]

Communism "has the pride of infallibility."[19] All who oppose the Communist "creed" (this expression is used by Engels)[20] are excommunicated. Marx wrote, "Bakunin should beware. Otherwise we will excommunicate him."[21]

Those who die in the service of Marxism are feasted as "martyrs." Marxism also has its sacraments: the solemn receptions in the toddlers' organization called "the Children of October," the oaths given when received as "Pioneers," after which come the higher grades of initiation in the Komsomol and the Party. Confession is replaced with public self-criticism before the assembly of Party members.[22]

Marxism is a church. It has all the characteristics of a church. Yet, its god is not named in its popular literature. But, as seen by the proofs given in this book, Satan is obviously its god.

It is strange that though Marxism is clearly Satanic, it is not seen as a threat by many churches in the free world. Some illuminating statistics on this are available.

Seminary professors in the United States were asked, "Can an individual consistently be a good member of your denomination and adhere to Marxism?"

Below are the percentage figures of those who answered yes:[23]

Episcopalian	68%
Lutheran	53
Presbyterian	49
Methodist	49
Church of Christ	47
American Baptist	44
Roman Catholic	31

How sad that those who follow the Truth are duped by those who serve the father of lies.

7

MARX, DARWIN, AND REVOLUTION

Marx and Darwin

What was the specific contribution of Marx to Satan's plan for mankind?

The Bible teaches that God created man in His own image (Genesis 1:26). Up to the time of Marx, man continued to be considered as "the crown of creation." Marx was Satan's chosen tool to make man lose his self-esteem, his conviction that he comes from high places and is meant to return to them. Marxism is the first systematic and detailed philosophy that drastically reduces the notion of man.

According to Marx, man is primarily a belly that has to be filled and refilled constantly. The prevailing interests of man are economic in nature; he produces in order to satisfy his needs. For this purpose, he enters into social relationships with others. This is the basis of society, what Marx calls the infrastructure. Marriage, love, art, science, religion, philosophy, everything other than the

7

needs of the belly, are all superstructure, determined in the last analysis by the state of the belly.

No wonder Marx praised Darwin's book *The Descent of Man*, another masterstroke that makes men forget their divine origin and divine purpose. Darwin said that man springs from the animal world.

Man was dethroned by these two. Satan could not dethrone God, so he devalued man. Man was shown to be the progeny of animals and a mere servant to his intestines.

It is a strange coincidence that the nineteenth century gave the world three leading personalities opposed to Christianity, all bearing the name of Charles: Karl (German for Charles) Marx, Charles Darwin, and the French poet Charles Baudelaire. The latter wrote in "Abel and Cain":

> Race of Cain, ascend to heaven
> And throw God to the earth.

Marx wrote to Ferdinand Lassalle on January 16, 1861, "Darwin's book is very important and serves me as a basis in the natural sciences for the historical class struggle."

Marx's son-in-law, Paul Lafargue, in *Socialism and the Intellectuals*, says,

> When Darwin published his *Origin of Species*,
> he took away from God his role as creator in the

organic world, as Franklin has despoiled him of
his thunderbolt.

(It was not Darwin's original intent to harm religion. He had
written, "There is a grandeur in this view of life, with its several
powers, having been originally breathed into a few forms or into
one." In order to make his position more emphatic, Darwin
inserted the phrase "by the Creator" after "breathed" in the second edition. It remained there in all the succeeding editions he
published.)

Later Freud would complete the work of these two giants,
reducing man basically to a sex urge, sometimes sublimated in
politics, art, or religion. It was the Swiss psychologist Carl Gustav
Jung who returned to the biblical doctrine that the religious
impulse is man's basic urge.

The age of Marx was a time of Satanist ferment in many
spheres of life. The Russian poet Sologub wrote, "My father is the
Devil." Another Russian poet, Briusov, said, "I glorify equally the
Lord and the Devil."

Marx was a child of the time that gave us Nietzsche (Hitler's
and Mussolini's favorite philosopher), Max Stirner, an extreme
anarchist, and Oscar Wilde, the first theoretician of freedom for
homosexuality, a vice that today has met with acceptance even
among the clergy.

Satanic forces prepared Russia for the victory of Marxism.
The time of the revolution was a period when love, goodwill, and
healthy feelings were considered mean and retrograde. Girls hid

their innocence and husbands their faithfulness. Destruction was praised as good taste, neurasthenia as the sign of a fine mind. This was the theme of new writers who burst on the scene out of obscurity. Men invented vices and perversions, and were fastidious in their avoidance of being thought moral.

How was it that Stalin became a revolutionist after reading Darwin?[1] As a student in an Orthodox seminary, he obtained from Darwin the concept that we are not creatures of God, but the result of an evolution in which ruthless competition reigns. It is only the strongest and most cruel who survive. He learned that moral and religious criteria play no role in nature and that man is as much a part of nature as a fish or an ape. Long live ruthlessness and cruelty!

Darwin had written a scientific book setting forth his theory of origins. It had no economic or political implications. But though many might go so far as to suggest that God created the world through a long process of evolution, the end result of Darwin's theory has been the killing of tens of millions of innocents. He therefore became the spiritual father of the greatest mass-murderer in history.

Beyond the intellectual turmoil of the nineteenth century can be traced the influence of the French Revolution, which was spiritually very much akin to the Russian cataclysm of the twentieth century.

During the upheaval in France, Anarchasis Clootz, a leading French revolutionary and Illuminatus, declared himself to be "the personal enemy of Jesus Christ."[2] He proclaimed before the Convention of November 17, 1792, "The people is the sovereign and the god of the world…. Only fools believe in any other God, in a Supreme Being." The Convention then issued a decree proclaiming "the nullification of all religions."

For those of us who take seriously the words of the Lord's Prayer, "Deliver us from evil" (Matthew 6:13), the meaning is clear: we implore a loving God to protect us and society around us from false doctrine, from pernicious art that accustoms us to evil under the guise of beauty, and from immorality in life. Then we need have no fear of the devil's snares.

You have a choice: Do you want to become like the devil, cruel and vicious, or like Jesus, the God-man of holy love and peace?

Moses Hess's False Zionism

To complete the picture, we will consider Moses Hess, the man who converted Marx and Engels to the Socialist ideal.

There is a tombstone in Israel inscribed with the words, "Moses Hess, founder of the German Social-Democrat Party." Hess expounds his beliefs in the *Red Catechism for the German People:*

> What is black? Black is the clergy…. These theologians are the worst aristocrats…. The clergyman teaches the princes to oppress the people in the name of God. Secondly, he teaches the people to allow themselves to be oppressed and exploited in God's name. Thirdly and principally, he provides for himself with God's help a splendid life

on earth, while the people are advised to wait for heaven.

The Red flag symbolizes the permanent revolution until the completed victory of the working classes in all civilized countries: the Red republic.... The Socialist revolution is my religion.... The workers, when they have conquered one country, must help their brethren in the rest of the world.[3]

This was Hess's religion when he first issued the *Catechism.* In the second edition, he added a few chapters. This time the same religion, i.e., the Socialist revolution, uses Christian language in order to accredit itself with believers. Together with the propaganda of revolution, there are indeed a few nice words about Christianity as a religion of love and humanity. But its message must be made clearer: its hell must not be on earth and its heaven beyond. The Socialist society will be the true fulfillment of Christianity. Thus Satan disguises himself as an angel of light.

After Hess convinced Marx and Engels of the Socialist idea, claiming from the very beginning that its purpose would be to give "the last kick to medieval religion"[4] (his friend Georg Jung said it even more clearly: "Marx will surely chase God from his heaven"[5]), an interesting development took place in Hess's life. He who had founded modern socialism also founded an entirely different movement, a specific brand of Zionism.

Thus Hess, founder of a socialism whose aim was to "chase God from heaven," was also founder of a diabolic type of Zionism that was to destroy godly Zionism, the Zionism of love, understanding, and concord with surrounding nations. He who taught Marx the importance of class struggle wrote in 1862 these surprising words: "Race struggle is primary, class struggle is secondary."[6]

He had lighted the fire of class war, a fire never extinguished, instead of teaching people to cooperate for the common good. The same Hess then breeds a distorted Zionism, a Zionism of race struggle. As we reject Satanic Marxism, so also must every responsible Jew or Christian reject this diabolical perversion of Zionism.

Hess claims Jerusalem for the Jews, but without Jesus, the King of the Jews. What need has Hess of Jesus? He writes,

> Every Jew has the making of a Messiah in himself,
> every Jewess that of a Mater Delorosa in herself.[7]

Then why in the world did he not make of the Jew Marx a Messiah, a God-anointed man, instead of a hater bent on chasing God from heaven? For Hess, Jesus is "a Jew, whom the heathen deified as their Savior."[8] Neither Hess nor the Jews seem to need Him for themselves.

Hess does not wish to be saved himself, and for an individual to seek personal sanctification is "Indo-German," he says. The aim of the Jews, according to him, must be "a Messianic state," "to prepare mankind for the revelation of the divine essence,"[9] which means, as he acknowledges in his *Red Catechism,* to wage the Socialist revolution through racial and class struggle.

Moses Hess, who allotted to his idol Marx the task of putting an end to medieval religion, replacing it with the religion of Socialist revolution, writes these amazing words: "I have always been edified by Hebrew prayers."[10] What prayers do those who consider religion the opiate of the people say? We have seen already that the founder of scientific atheism prayed while wearing phylacteries before burning candles. Jewish prayers can be misused in a blasphemous sense, just as Christian prayers are perverted in Satanist ritual.

Hess had taught Marx that socialism was inseparable from internationalism. Marx writes in his *Communist Manifesto* that the proletariat has no fatherland. In his *Red Catechism* Hess mocks the fatherland notion of the Germans, and he would have done the same with the fatherland notion of any other European nation. Hess criticized the Erfurt program of the German Social-Democrat Party for its unconditional recognition of the national principle. But Hess is an internationalist with a difference: Jewish patriotism must remain. He writes,

> Whoever denies Jewish nationalism is not only
> an apostate, a renegade in the religious sense, but
> a traitor to his people and to his family. Should
> it prove true that the emancipation of the Jews
> is incompatible with Jewish nationalism, then

> the Jew must sacrifice emancipation…. The Jew
> must be, above all, a Jewish patriot.[11]

I agree with Hess's patriotic ideas to the extent that what is sauce for the goose is sauce for the gander. I am for every kind of patriotism—that of the Jews, the Arabs, the Germans, the Russians, the Americans. Patriotism is a virtue if it means the endeavor to promote economically, politically, spiritually, and religiously the welfare of one's own nation, provided that it is done in friendship and cooperation with other nations. But the Jewish patriotism of a revolutionary Socialist who denies the patriotism of all other nations is highly suspect. This seems to be a diabolical plan to make all peoples hate the Jews.

If I were a non-Jew who saw the Jews accept Hess's plan of unilateral patriotism, I would oppose it. Fortunately, no Jews have accepted this Satanic plan. In fact, it was Herzl who gave a sane turn to Zionism. In its modern form no trace of Satanism has remained.

The race struggle proposed by Hess is false, as false as the class struggle he enjoined.

Hess did not abandon socialism for this specific kind of Zionism. After writing *Rome and Jerusalem,* he continued to be active in the world Socialist movement.

Hess does not state his thoughts clearly; therefore it is difficult to evaluate them. It is enough to know that according to him, "the Christian world views Jesus as a Jewish saint who became a pagan man."[12] It is enough for us to read in his book, "We today long for a far more comprehensive salvation than that which Christianity was ever able to offer."[13] From *The Red Catechism* it follows that this more comprehensive salvation is the Socialist revolution.

No one can be a Christian without loving the Jews. Jesus was Jewish, as were the virgin Mary and all the apostles. The Bible is Jewish. The Lord has said, "Salvation is from the Jews" (John 4:22). Hess, on the other hand, exalted the Jews as though he consciously wanted to create a violent anti-Jewish reaction. He said that his religion was that of Socialist revolution. The clergy of all "other" religions were crooks. Revolution was the only religion for which Hess had a high regard. He writes,

> Our religion [the Jewish] has as its point of departure the enthusiasm of a race which from its appearance on the stage of history has foreseen the final purposes of mankind and which had a foreboding of the messianic time in which the spirit of humanity will be fulfilled, not only in this or that individual or only partially, but in the social institutions of all mankind.[14]

This time—which Hess calls "messianic"—is the time of the victory of the Socialist world revolution. The idea that the Jewish religion had as its point of departure the concept of a godless Socialist revolution is an ugly joke and an insult to the Jewish people.

Hess speaks persistently in religious terms, but he does not believe in God. He writes that "our God is nothing more than the human race united in love."[15] The way to arrive at such a union is the Socialist revolution, in which tens of millions of specimens of his beloved mankind will be tortured and killed.

He makes no secret of the fact that he wishes neither the domination of heaven, nor that of earthly powers, which are both oppressive. There is no good in any religion, except that of social revolution.

> It is useless and inefficient to elevate the people to real freedom and to make them participate in the goods of existence, without freeing them from spiritual slavery, i.e., from religion.[16]

He speaks in one breath about "the absolutism of celestial and earthly tyrants over slaves."[17]

The Satanic depths of communism can be understood only by knowing the kind of man Moses Hess was, for he influenced Marx and Engels, with whom he founded the First International, as well as Bakunin. Without a knowledge of Hess, Marx is unintelligible, because it is he who brought Marx to socialism.

Consider Marx's words already quoted:

> Words I teach all mixed up into a devilish muddle. Thus, anyone may think just what he chooses to think.[18]

Marx wrote in such a manner. Hess's writings are an even more devilish muddle, which are difficult to untangle but which must be analyzed for possible connections between Marx and Satanism.

Hess's first book was called *The Holy History of Mankind.* He proclaimed it to be "a work of the holy spirit of truth,"[19] saying further that as the Son of God freed men from their own slavery, Hess would free them from political bondage. "I am called to witness for the light, as John has been."[20]

At that time Marx, who was still opposed to socialism and had not known Hess personally, started to write a book against him. For unknown reasons, this book was never completed. He later became Hess's disciple.[21]

As previously indicated, Hess's avowed aims were to give a last kick to medieval religion and to produce ravages. In the introduction to his book *Last Judgment,* he declares his satisfaction that the German philosopher Kant had allegedly "decapitated the old Father Jehovah together with the whole holy family."[22] (Hess covers his own ideas with the name of the great philosopher. Kant had had no such intentions. He had written to the contrary: "I had to limit knowledge to make place for faith."[23])

Hess declares the Jewish as well as the Christian religion to be "dead,"[24] which does not prevent him from writing in *Rome and Jerusalem* about "our holy writings," "the holy language of our fathers," "our cult," "the divine laws," "the ways of Providence," and "godly life."[25]

It is not that at different stages in life he held different opinions. In his pseudo-Zionist book he declares that he does not disown his former godless endeavors. No, this is an intentional "devilish muddle."[26]

Hess was Jewish and a forerunner of Zionism. Because Hess, Marx, and other people like them were Jewish, some people consider communism a Jewish plot. Yet Marx also wrote an anti-Jewish book. In this respect, too, he has simply followed Hess.

This "Zionist," Hess, who elevates Jewry to heaven, wrote in his book *About the Monetary System:*

> The Jews, who had the role, in the natural history of the social animal world, to develop mankind into a savage animal, have fulfilled this, their professional job. The mystery of Judaism and Christianity has been revealed in the modern Judeo-Christian. The mystery of the blood of Christ, like the mystery of the old Jewish worship of the blood, appears here unveiled as being the mystery of the predatory animal.[27]

Don't worry if you fail to understand these words. They were written "mixed up into a devilish muddle," but the hatred for Jewishness contained in them is clear. Hess is a racist, Jewish as well as anti-Jewish, according to the needs of the spirit that inspired his works and that he calls "holy."

Hitler could have learned his racism from Hess. He who had taught Marx that social class is a decisive factor also wrote the contrary: "Life is an immediate product of race."[28] Social institutions

and conceptions, as well as religions, are typical and original
creations of the race. The problem of race lies hidden behind all
the problems of nationalities and freedom. All past history was
concerned with the struggle of races and classes. Race struggle is
primary; class struggle is secondary.[29]

How will Hess manage to have so many contradictory ideas
triumph?

> I will use the sword against all citizens who resist
> the endeavors of the proletariat.[30]

We will hear the same from Marx:

> Violence is the midwife which takes the new soci-
> ety out of the womb of the old one.[31]

Marx's first teacher was the philosopher Hegel, who merely
paved the way for Hess. Marx, too, had sucked poison from Hegel,
for whom Christianity was wretched in comparison to the glorious
past of Greek culture. Hegel wrote, "Christians have piled up such
a heap of reasons for comfort in misfortune…that we ought to be
sorry in the end that we cannot lose a father or a mother once a
week," while for the Greek "misfortune was misfortune, pain was
pain."[32]

Christianity had been satirized in Germany before Hegel. But
he was the first to satirize Jesus Himself. He also wrote nice things
about Christianity, the same "devilish muddle."

We are what we feed upon. Marx fed upon Satanic ideas; therefore he set forth Satanist doctrine.

The Organization "Hell"

Communists have a habit of creating front organizations. All of the above suggests the probability that Communist movements are themselves front organizations for occult Satanism. The means to fight Satanism are spiritual, not carnal; otherwise, while one Satanist front organization, such as Nazism, is defeated, another will rise to greater victory.

Himmler, the minister of interior affairs of Nazi Germany, thought himself to be King Henry the Fowler's reincarnation. He believed that it was possible to harness occult powers to serve the Nazi army. Several Nazi leaders were involved in black magic.

What was mere supposition when I published the first edition of this present book is now a proven fact. The proof has been given by the Communists themselves. The story begins with the Netchaiev case, which prompted Dostoyevski to write his renowned novel *The Demons*.

Netchaiev, called a "splendid, young fanatic"[33] by Bakunin, Marx's collaborator in founding the First International, wrote *The Catechism of the Revolutionist* as the guide for the Russian organization "Popular Revenge." It appeared around 1870.

The purpose of this organization was formulated as follows:

> Our cause is terrible, complete, universal, and pitiless destruction.... Let us unite with the savage,

criminal world, these true and only revolutionists of Russia.[34]

The first man the Netchaiev group killed was one of their founding comrades, Ivanov, who dared to criticize his leadership. No criticism was permitted.

Netchaiev's plan was to divide mankind into two unequal parts:

> One tenth gets personal liberty and unlimited rights over the other nine tenths. These must lose their personality and turn into a kind of herd.[35]

> They will engage in spy work. Each member of society will spy on the other and will be obliged to denounce.... All are slaves and are equal in slavery.[36]

Netchaiev wrote in his *Catechism:*

> A revolutionist must infiltrate everywhere, in the upper and lower classes...in churches...in literature.[37]

His disciple Peter Verhovensky commented:

> We are already terribly powerful.... Jurors who
> acquit criminals are completely ours. The district
> attorney who trembles in courts not to be consid-
> ered liberal enough is ours. Administrators, men
> of letters, we are many, very many, and they don't
> know they belong to us.[38]

On the basis of such a program an organization with an impressive name was formed: the World Revolutionist League. Its constitution was signed by Netchaiev and Bakunin, Marx's intimate collaborator.[39] In the beginning the League consisted of only a handful of men.

The revolutionist Duke Peter Dolgorukov wrote on October 31, 1862,

> In London I met Kelsiev [who belonged to the
> above organization], a narrow-minded but good
> man, terribly fanatical, with the face of a soft
> man. Kelsiev told me softly, with a benevolent
> look: "If we have to slaughter, why not slaughter,
> provided this is useful?"...All these London men
> speak continually about "burning down, slaugh-
> tering, cutting in pieces." These words have never
> left their tongue since Bakunin came to England.

In 1869, in Geneva, Netchaiev wrote a proclamation in which, referring to the man who shot Emperor Alexander II, he advises:

We must consider what Karakazov did as prologue. Yes, this was a prologue. Let us see to it
that the drama itself begins soon.[40]

Another proclamation says,

Soon, soon the day comes when we will unfurl
the great flag of the future, the Red flag, and we
will attack with great noise the Imperial palace....

We will have one shout, "To the axes!" and
then we will kill the party of the emperor. Do not
pity.... Kill in public places if these base rascals
dare to enter them, kill in houses, kill in villages.

Remember, those who will not side with us
will be against us. Whoever is against us is our
enemy. And we must destroy enemies by all
means.[41]

In 1872, a revolutionary society was formed under the simple
name "The Organization," which had a super-secret circle chill-
ingly called "Hell." Though its goals have continued to be pursued
for well over a century by groups that continually change their
names, its existence has been unknown to the outside world.

Soviet historians have dared to write about the activities of
"Hell," a forerunner of the Russian Communist Party, only as
recently as 1965, ninety-three years after its formation.

In *Revolutionist Underground in Russia*, E. S. Vilenskaia wrote,

> "Hell" was the name of the center above the secret organization, which not only used terror against the monarchy, but also had punitive functions toward the members of the secret organization.[42]

In *Tchernishevsky or Netchaiev*,[43] we read that one of the members (Fediseev) of "Hell" took it upon himself to poison his own father in order to give the organization his inheritance. Here are some of the expressed aims of this Satanic organization:

> Mystification is the best, almost the only means to impel men to make a revolution.

> It is enough to kill a few million people and the wheels of revolution will be oiled.

> Our ideal is awful, complete, universal, and pitiless destruction.

In their writings we constantly find the words, "We are not afraid." A typical example is the following proclamation by Tchernishevsky, who belonged to this movement:

We are not afraid that we might find out three
times more blood will have to be shed for the
overthrow of the existing order than the Jacobins
[French revolutionists] had to shed in their
revolution in 1790.... If for the fulfillment of
our objectives we had to slaughter one hundred
thousand landlords, we would not be afraid of
this either.[44]

In reality, the number of victims was much greater. Churchill
says in his *Memoirs of World War II* that Stalin confessed that ten
million people died as a result of the collectivization of agriculture
in the Soviet Union.

The important fact to remember is that the Communists have
now confessed, after a delay of almost a hundred years, that at
the inception of their movement was a circle called "Hell." Why
"Hell"? Why not "The Society for the Betterment of the Poor" or
"…of Mankind"? Why the stark emphasis on hell?

Today the Communists are more cautious. But in the beginning their very name revealed that their avowed aim was to recruit
men for eternal damnation.

ANGELS OF LIGHT

The Satanist Mass

Anton LaVey, founder of the Church of Satan, documented fundamental Satanist teachings in his *The Satanic Bible*. The "Bible" opens with the "Book of Satan," an "infernal diatribe" through which Satan himself is allowed to "speak out in the same manner as the spokesmen of the Lord of the Righteous" and to "shout back" at Christians and God.[1]

In the opening lines of the "Book of Satan," Satan says, "I stand forth to challenge the wisdom of the world; to interrogate the 'laws' of man and of 'God'!"[2] As Satan establishes his challenge to God, he continues:

> I request reasons for your golden rule and ask
> the why and wherefore of your ten commands.
> Before none of your printed idols do I bend in
> acquiescence, and he who said "thou shalt" to
> me is my mortal foe!

> I dip my forefinger in the watery blood of your
> impotent mad redeemer, and write over his
> thorn-torn brow: The TRUE prince of evil—the
> king of the slaves! Behold the crucifix, what does
> it symbolize? Pallid incompetence hanging on a
> tree.[3]

LaVey also details the ritual practices of Satanism in *The Satanic Rituals*, saying, "On the altar of the Devil up is down, pleasure is pain, darkness is light, slavery is freedom, and madness is sanity."[4]

In that work, he reveals "the actual texts of such forbidden rites as the Black Mass and Satanic Baptisms for both adults and children." In the Black Mass,[5] Satan is exalted as supreme:

> Before the mighty and ineffable Prince of Dark-
> ness, and in the presence of all the dread demons
> of the Pit…we proclaim that Satan-Lucifer rules
> the earth, and we ratify and renew our promise to
> recognize and honor Him in all things…

As the ritual continues, the priest calls forward a nun who is presented with a chamber pot. She then urinates into the pot and passes it to the other participants. As she does this, a deacon speaks, attributing to Satan the divine attributes that Scripture reserves for the one true God:

> She maketh the font resound with the tears of
> her mortification.

The waters of her shame become a shower of
blessing in the tabernacle of Satan....
And the Dark Lord shall wipe all tears from
her eyes, for He said unto me: It is done. I am
Alpha and Omega, the beginning and the end.
I will give freely unto him that is athirst of the
fountain of the water of life.

The priest then leads the participants in a perversion of the
Lord's Prayer:

Our Father which art in Hell,
hallowed be Thy name.
Thy kingdom is come, Thy will is done;
on earth as it is in Hell!
We take this night our rightful due,
and trespass not on paths of pain.
Lead us unto temptation,
and deliver us from false piety,
for Thine is the kingdom and the power and the
glory forever!

The ceremony culminates in a defamation of the Eucharist,
during which the priest takes a wafer and states:

...O lasting foulness of Bethlehem, we would
have thee confess thy impudent cheats, thy
inexpiable crimes! We would drive deeper the

nails into thy hands, press down the crown of
thorns upon thy brow, and bring blood from the
dry wounds of thy sides.

And this we can and *will* do by violating the
quietude of thy body, profaner of the ample
vices, abstractor of stupid purities, cursed
Nazarene, impotent king, fugitive god!
Behold, great Satan, this symbol of the flesh
of him who would purge the Earth of pleasure
and who, in the name of Christian "justice" has
caused the death of millions of our honored
Brothers. We curse and defile his name.

O Infernal Majesty, condemn him to the Pit,
evermore to suffer in perpetual anguish.
Bring Thy wrath upon him, O Prince of
Darkness, and rend him that he may know the
extent of Thy anger.
…Vanish into nothingness, thou fool of fools,
thou vile and abhorred pretender to the majesty
of Satan!
Vanish into the void of thy empty Heaven,
for thou wert never, nor shalt thou ever be.

The wafer, in representation of Christ's body, is then defiled
and thrown to the ground where the priest and others trample it,
in a definitive act portraying Satan's dominion and authority.

Friedrich Nietzsche, in the fourth part of *Thus Spake Zarathustra*, under "Awakening," provides the text of another black mass he himself composed. Its spirit does not differ much from the one above.[6]

Public black masses are rare today, but Stefan Zweig in his biography of Fouché describes one held in Lyon during the French Revolution.

A revolutionary, Chalier, had been killed, and the black mass was celebrated in his honor. On that day crucifixes were torn from all the altars and priestly robes were confiscated. A huge crowd of men carrying a bust of the revolutionary descended on the marketplace. Three proconsuls were there to honor Chalier, "the God-Savior who died for the people."

The crowd carried chalices, holy images, and utensils used in the mass. Behind them was an ass wearing a bishop's mitre on its head. A crucifix and a Bible had been tied to its tail.

In the end, the Gospel was thrown into the fire together with missals, prayerbooks, and icons. The ass was made to drink from a Communion chalice as a reward for its blasphemous services. The bust of Chalier was put on an altar in place of the smashed image of Christ. Tens of former Catholic priests participated.

A medal was issued to commemorate this event. Secret black masses do not take this shape, but the spirit is basically the same.

The Russian magazine *Yuni Kommunist* describes in detail a Satanist mass in which bread and wine, mixed with dung and tears taken from operating on the eyes of a living cock, are "transubstantiated" into the alleged body and blood of Lucifer.

During this ceremony the words of the mass are read from the end to the beginning, as is customary in Satanist rituals. Then a covenant is concluded between Satan and his worshipers. The points of the contract are: renunciation of Christian teaching; new baptism in the name of the devil, with a change of name; renunciation of godparents, with the substitution of other protectors; bringing some personal clothing as a gift to Satan; swearing loyalty to Satan while standing in a magic circle; inscription of the new member's name in "The Book of the Dead," as opposed to Christ's Book of Life; the promise to consecrate one's children to the devil, as well as gifts and deeds pleasing to him; an oath to keep the secrets of the witches' coven and to demean the Christian religion.

Why would Communists dig out such teachings from old books of demonology and recommend them to the youth, saying, "They are rich food for thought"? Is that all that Marxism has to offer the human mind?

The Communist magazine continues:

> In this devilish antiworld, which externally is completely like ours, man must reply with evil to every success in life.

Then it brazenly affirms the following as the slogan of Satanism: "Satan is not the foe of man. He is Life, Love, Light."

The article ends with a quotation from Uspenskii expressing the hope of the Communists:

> There are ideas which touch the most intimate
> corners of our lives. Once these are touched, the
> marks remain forever.... They will poison life.[7]

This insidious material is presented in a subtle manner as if to provide information, but its real aim is to arouse the reader's morbid curiosity, with ravaging effects.

During the initiation ceremony for the third degree in the Satanist church, the initiate has to take the oath, "I will always do only what I will." In other words, there is no authority beyond the polluted self. This is an open denial of God's commandment "not to follow after your own heart and your own eyes, which you are inclined to whore after" (Numbers 15:39).

Marxists appeal to the basest passions, stirring up envy toward the rich and violence toward everyone. "It is the evil side which makes history," wrote Marx, and he played a major role in shaping history.

Revolutions do not cause love to triumph. Rather, killing becomes a mania. In the Russian and Chinese revolutions, after the Communists had murdered tens of millions of innocents, they could not stop murdering and brutally killed one another.

Is Everything Permitted?

The Satanist cult is very old, older than Christianity. The prophet Isaiah might have had it in view when he wrote, "We have turned—every one—to his own way; and the LORD has laid on him [the Savior] the iniquity of us all" (Isaiah 53:6).

True religious feeling is at the opposite pole. Certain Hassidic rabbis never said "I," because they considered it a pronoun that belonged only to God. His will is binding on human behavior.

By contrast, when a man or woman is initiated into the seventh degree of Satanism, he swears that his principle will be, "Nothing is true, and everything is permitted." When Marx filled out a quiz game for his daughter, he answered the question "Which is your favorite principle?" with the words, "Doubt everything."[8]

Marx wrote in *The Communist Manifesto* that his aim was the abolition not only of all religions, but also of all morals, which would make everything permissible.

It was with a sense of horror that I read the mystery of the seventh degree of Satanism inscribed on a poster at the University of Paris during the 1968 riots. It had been simplified to the formula, "It is forbidden to forbid," which is the natural consequence of "Nothing is true, and everything is permissible."

The youth obviously did not realize the stupidity of the formula. If it is forbidden to forbid, it must also be forbidden to forbid forbidding. If everything is permissible, forbidding is permissible, too.

Young people think that permissiveness means liberty. Marxists know better. To them, the formula means that it is forbidden to forbid cruel dictatorships like those in Red China and the Soviet Union.

Dostoyevski had said it already: "If there is no God, everything is permitted." If there is no God, our instincts are free. The ultimate expression of this kind of liberty is hatred. Whoever is free in this sense considers lovingkindness a weakness of the spirit.

Engels said, "Generalized love of men is absurdity." The anarchist thinker Max Stirner, author of *The I and Its Property* and one of Marx's friends, wrote, "I am legitimately authorized to do everything I am capable of."

Communism is collective demon-possession. Solzhenitsyn in *The Gulag Archipelago* reveals some of its horrible results in the souls and lives of people.

The Mythical Marx

Let me say again that I am conscious that the evidence I have given to date may be considered circumstantial. But what I have written is enough to show that what Marxists say about Karl Marx is a myth. He was not prompted by concern for the poverty of his fellowmen, for which revolution was the only solution. He did not love the proletariat, but called them "nuts," "stupid," "asses," "rascals," even obscenities. He did not even love his comrades in the fight for communism. He called Freiligrath "the swine,"[9] Lassalle "Jewish n——r" [racial epithet deleted][10] Bakunin "a theoretical zero."[11]

A Lieutenant Tchekhov, a fighter in the revolution of 1848 who spent nights drinking with Marx, commented that Marx's narcissism had devoured everything good that had been in him.

Marx certainly did not love mankind. Giuseppe Mazzini, who knew him well, wrote that he had "a destructive spirit. His heart bursts with hatred rather than with love toward men."[12]

Mazzini was himself a "Carbonari." This organization, founded in 1815 by Maghella, a Genoan Freemason, declared its "final aim to be that of Voltaire and of the French Revolution—the complete

annihilation of Catholicism and ultimately of Christianity."
It began as an Italian operation, but subsequently developed a
broader European orientation.

Though Mazzini was critical of Marx, he maintained his
friendship with him. *The Jewish Encyclopedia* says that Mazzini and
Marx were entrusted with the task of preparing the address and
the constitution of the First International. This means that they
were birds of the same feather, though they sometimes pecked at
each other.

I know of no testimonies from Marx's contemporaries that
contradict Mazzini's evaluation. Marx the loving man is a myth
constructed only after his death.

In fact, his favorite bit of verse was this quotation from
G. Werth: "There is nothing more beautiful in the world than to
bite one's enemies." In his own words, he said outright, "We are
pitiless. We ask for no pity. When our turn comes, we will not
shun terrorism." These are hardly the sentiments of a lover.

Marx did not hate religion because it stood in the way of the
happiness of mankind. On the contrary, he simply wanted to make
mankind unhappy in this world and throughout eternity. He proclaimed this as his ideal. His avowed aim was the destruction of
religion. Socialism, concern for the proletariat, humanism—these
were only pretexts.

After Marx had read *The Origin of Species* by Charles Darwin,
he wrote a letter to Lassalle in which he exults that God—in the
natural sciences at least—had been given "the death blow."[13] What
idea, then, preempted all others in Marx's mind? Was it the plight
of the poor proletariat? If so, of what possible value was Darwin's

theory? The only tenable conclusion is that Marx's chief aim was the destruction of religion.

The good of the workers was only a pretense. Where proletarians do not fight for Socialist ideals, Marxists will exploit racial differences or the so-called generation gap. The main thing is, religion must be destroyed.

Marx believed in hell. And his program, the driving force in his life, was to send men to hell.

Robin Goodfellow

Marx wrote,

> In the signs that bewilder the middle class, the
> aristocracy, and the prophets of regression, we
> recognize our brave friend, Robin Goodfellow,
> the old mole that can work in the earth so fast—
> the revolution.[14]

Scholars who have read this apparently never looked into the identity of this Robin Goodfellow, Marx's brave friend, the worker for revolution.

The sixteenth-century evangelist William Tyndale used Robin Goodfellow as a name for the devil.[15] Shakespeare in his *Midsummer Night's Dream* called him "the knavish sprite that misleads night-wanderers, laughing at their harm."[16]

Thus, according to Marx, considered the father of communism, a demon was the author of the Communist revolution and was his personal friend.

Lenin's Tomb

In His revelation to the apostle John, Jesus said something very mysterious to the church in Pergamum (a city in Asia Minor): "I know where you dwell, where Satan's throne is" (Revelation 2:13). Pergamum (or Pergamon) was apparently a center of the Satanist cult in that period. Now the world-famous Baedeker tourist guidebooks for Berlin state that the Island Museum contained the Pergamum altar of Zeus until 1944. German archaeologists had excavated it, and it had been in the center of the Nazi capital during Hitler's Satanist regime.

But the saga of the seat of Satan is not yet over. *Svenska Dagbladet* (Stockholm) for January 27, 1948, reveals that the architect Alexei Shchusev (or Stjusev), who built Lenin's mausoleum, used this altar of Satan as a model for the mausoleum in 1924.[17]

Many visitors wait in line every day to visit this sanctuary of Satan in which Lenin's mummy lies in state. Religious leaders of the whole world pay their homage to the Marxist "patron saint" in this monument erected to Satan.

The Satanist temple at Pergamum was only one of the many of its kind. Why did Jesus single it out? Probably not because of the minor role it played at that time. Rather, His words were prophetic. He spoke about Nazism and communism, through which this altar would be honored.

It is worth noting with irony that on the grave of Lenin's father there stood a cross with the inscription "The light of Christ illuminates all" and a multitude of Bible verses.

9

WHOM WILL WE SERVE?

A Call for Action

This book has been written in an exploratory manner. Christian thinkers, like other scholars, often succumb to the temptation to prove preconceived ideas. They do not necessarily present only the truth as far as they have ascertained it. Sometimes they are prone to stretch the truth or exaggerate their argumentation in order to prove their point.

I do not claim to have provided indisputable proof that Marx was a member of a sect of devil-worshipers, but I believe that there are sufficient leads to imply this strongly. There are certainly enough leads to suggest Satanic influence upon his life and teachings, while conceding that there are gaps in a chain of evidence that would lead to a definite conclusion in this matter. I have provided the initial impulse. I pray that others will also continue this important inquiry into the relationship between Marxism and Satanism.

Meanwhile, how can the church defeat Marxism?

The secular anti-Communist world can use weapons of economic sanctions, political pressure, military threats, and broad-based propaganda. The church should certainly support any actions conscience can endorse in the battle against the enemies of God. But it also has a weapon of its own.

The Ukrainian Metropolitan of the Catholic Church, Byzantine rite, Andrew Count Sheptytsky, once requested that Rome order prayers of exorcism against the Communists, whose "regime cannot be explained except by a massive possession of the Devil."

Jesus did not tell His disciples to complain about demons, but to cast them out (Matthew 10:8). I believe this can be effectively accomplished, though this book cannot enter into details about such prayer.

Readers React

The first edition of this book produced interesting responses. Many greeted it as a new discovery in the understanding of Marxism and gave me valuable hints as to where I could find new material.

On the other hand, a Dutch personality dedicated several columns of his theological magazine to minimizing the importance of the discovery. "Well," he says, "Marx may have indulged in black magic, but this does not count for much. All men are sinners, all men have evil thoughts. Let us not be alarmed at this."

It is true that all men are sinners, but not all are criminals. All men are sinners, but some are murderers and some are righteous judges who pass judgment on them.

The crimes of communism are unequaled. What other political system has killed sixty million men in half a century?[1] Another sixty million have been killed in Red China. (Some estimates run much higher.)

There are degrees of sinfulness and criminality. The enormity of crime is a measure of the intensity of Satanic influence on the founder of modern communism. The sins of Marxism, like those of Nazism, surpass the ordinary. They are Satanic indeed.

I have also had letters from Satanists offering an apology for their religion. One of them writes:

> A defense of Satanism needs only the Bible for documentary evidence. Think of all the thousands of earthly people, created in God's own image, mind you, destroyed by fire and brimstone (Sodom and Gomorrah), a lethal miscellany of plagues, and, to top everything off, the drowning of the earth's population, except for Noah's family. All of these devastations brought about by a "merciful" God/Lord/Jehovah. What could a merciless god have done?
>
> But in all the Bible there is no record of even one death being brought about by Satan! So, let's hear it for Satan!

This Satanist has not studied the Bible well. Death came into the world through Satan's deceit, his luring Eve into sin, affecting all of humanity. This Satanist has also drawn his conclusions too soon. God has not yet finished with His creation.

Initially every painting is a senseless, often ugly mixture of lines and dots of many colors. It took da Vinci twenty years to make of these the beautiful *Mona Lisa*. God also creates in time. In time He shapes beings and destroys them to give them a new form. The seed that has neither beauty nor fragrance dies as seed in order to become a splendid, perfumed flower. Caterpillars have to die as such in order to become beautiful butterflies. Men are allowed by God to pass through the refining fires of suffering and death. The apotheosis of creation will be a new heaven and a new earth in which righteousness will triumph. Then those who have followed Satan will have to suffer an eternity of regrets.

Jesus endured flogging and crucifixion. But whoever wants to know God must look beyond the tomb to Jesus' resurrection and ascension. In contrast, the enemies of Jesus who plotted His death brought their people and their temple to destruction and lost their own souls.

Our critic wished to comprehend God through reason, which is not the right instrument for a creature. God cannot be comprehended by the mind, but only apprehended by a believing heart.

A Jamaican asked if the America that exploits his country is not as Satanic as Marx. It is not. Americans are sinners, as are all men. America has a small group of devil-worshipers. But the American nation as such does not worship the devil.

Nauka I Religia, the principal atheist magazine of Moscow, contained a long article written by two philosophers, Belov and Shilkin. They said that

> Wurmbrand's temperament might be envied by the greatest football players. His shouting is savage. This fighter calls for a crusade against socialism, which he calls an offspring of Satan. He was imprisoned in Romania for distributing religious literature instigating revolt against the government![2]

In this article two things are to be noted. First, I am called a "devilish pastor" for my book *Was Karl Marx a Satanist?* though the authors cannot produce one single fact to refute the documentation supporting Marx's links with a Satanist sect. Second, the article congratulates Christian leaders, even anticommunists, who have taken a stand against me. They might be adversaries of communism, but as long as they oppose Wurmbrand, chief enemy of communism, they were approved by Moscow.

One remarkable letter came from a Nigerian who had been a Marxist labor union leader for twenty years. My writings helped him to see that he had been led astray by Satan. Furthermore, he has become a Christian.

10

MARX OR CHRIST?

A Word to Marxists

If I were to address a rank-and-file Marxist, I would express the following concerns:

Many Marxists today are not animated by the spirit that controlled Hess, Marx, or Engels. They really love mankind; they are confident they are enrolled in an army fighting for universal good. It is not their desire to be tools of some weird Satanist sect.

Sadly, Satanic Marxism has a materialistic philosophy that blinds its followers to spiritual realities. But matter is not all that exists. There is a reality of the spirit, of truth, beauty, and ideals.

There is also a world of evil spirits, whose head is Satan. He fell from heaven through pride and drew down with him a host of angels. Then he seduced the progenitors of the human race. Since the Fall, his deceit has been perpetuated and increased through every conceivable device, until today we see God's beautiful creation ravaged by world wars, bloody revolutions and counterrevolutions, dictatorships, exploitation, racism of many kinds, false religions, agnosticism and atheism, crimes and crooked dealings, infidelities in love and friendship, broken marriages, rebellious children.

Mankind has lost the vision of God. But what has taken the place of this vision? Is it something better?

Man must and will have some kind of religion. It is his nature to worship. If he has not a God-fearing religion, he will have the religion of Satan and will persecute those who do not worship his "god."

Presumably only a few top leaders of communism have been and are consciously Satanists, but there is also an unconscious Satanism. A man can be a Satanist without being aware that such a religion exists. But if he hates the notion of God and the name of Christ, if he lives as though he were only matter, if he denies religious and moral principles, he is in fact a Satanist. Those who delve into the occult are in the same class.

On Sundays in Frankfurt, West Germany, more people go to spiritualist meetings, where the dead are allegedly called up, than to church services. There are known Satanist churches in Munich and Dusseldorf, for instance.[1] There are many such churches in France, Britain, the United States, and other countries as well.

In Great Britain there are thirty-five thousand practicing witches. American universities and even high schools offer courses in witchcraft, astrology, voodoo, magic, and ESP. In France forty thousand black masses are conducted annually.

Human beings may forsake God, but God has never forsaken His creatures. He sent into the world His only Son, Jesus Christ, to save the race of man. Incarnate love and compassion lived on earth in the life of a poor Jewish child, then of a humble carpenter, and eventually of a teacher of righteousness. Downtrodden man cannot save himself, any more than a drowning man can fetch himself out of the water. So Jesus, full of understanding for our inner conflicts, took upon Himself all our sins, including the sins of Marx and his followers, and bore the punishment for what we have done. He expiated our guilt by dying on a cross on Golgotha, after suffering the most terrible humiliation and agonizing pain.

Now we have His word that whoever puts faith in Him is forgiven and will live with Him in eternal paradise. Even notorious Marxists can be saved. It is worth noting that two Soviet Nobel prize winners, Boris Pasternak and Aleksandr Solzhenitsyn, both former Communists, after describing the extremities of crime to which Satanic Marxism leads, have confessed their faith in Christ. Svetlana Alliluyeva, the daughter of Stalin, the worst of the Marxist mass-murderers, also became a Christian.

Let us remember that Marx's ideal was to descend into the abyss of hell and draw all mankind in after him. Let us not follow him on this vicious path, but rather follow Christ who leads us upward to peaks of light, wisdom, and love, toward a heaven of unspeakable glory.

The Great Gulf

It is manifestly impossible to compare Jesus with Marx. Jesus belongs to an entirely different realm altogether.

Marx was human and probably a worshiper of the Evil One. Jesus is God and reduced Himself to the level of mankind in order to save it.

Marx proposed a human paradise. When the Soviets tried to implement it, the result was an inferno.

Jesus' kingdom is not of this world. It is a kingdom of love, righteousness, and truth. He calls to everyone, including Marxists and Satanists:

> Come to me, all who labor and are heavy laden,
> and I will give you rest. (Matthew 11:28)

All who believe in Him will have eternal life in His heavenly paradise.

There is no possibility of agreement between Christianity and Marxism, just as there can be no agreement between God and the devil. Jesus came to destroy the works of the Evil One (1 John 3:8). As Christians follow Him, they strive to destroy Marxism while retaining love for the individual Marxist and trying to win him to Christ.

Some proclaim that they are Marxist Christians. They are either deceivers or are deceived. One cannot be a Marxist Christian any more than one can be a devil-worshiping Christian.

Over the years, the Satanist aims of Marxism have not changed one bit. The Marxist philosopher Ernst Bloch writes in his book *Atheism in Christianity* that the seduction of the first human couple by the serpent opens the way of salvation for mankind. So man starts to become a god; it is the way of rebellion. Priestcraft and the possessors of goods repressed this truth. The original sin consists in the fact that man does not wish to be like God. Man must conquer the power. The theology of revolution wills it that man should conquer the power of God. The world must be changed in the image of man. There should be no heaven at all. The belief in a personal God is the fall into sin. This fall must be repaired.

There is a gulf between Christianity and communism that can be bridged only in one sense: Marxists must abandon their devil-inspired teacher, repent of their sins, and become followers of Jesus Christ.

Marxists are concerned with social and political problems, but these will have to be solved outside the tenets of Marxism. For Marx, socialism was only a pretense. His aim was to ruin mankind for eternity, a diabolical plan. By way of contrast, Christ desires our eternal salvation.

In the fight between Christianity and communism, believers "do not wrestle against flesh and blood, but against the rulers, against the authorities, against the cosmic powers over this present darkness, against the spiritual forces of evil in the heavenly places" (Ephesians 6:12).

Each of us has to choose not only between abstract good and abstract evil, but between God and Satan. Marx believed in God and hated Him. Even in his old age he worshiped Satan.

The average Marxist and the sympathizer of Marxism should not follow Marx in this spiritual aberration. Let us reject the bourgeois Marx, bearer of darkness, and Engels, factory owner and therefore, according to Marxist dogma, an exploiter. Let us rather choose the Light of the World and mankind's prime Benefactor, Jesus the working man, the Carpenter, the Savior, Lord of all.

"Proletarians of the World, Forgive Me!"

That Marxist Satanism has ravaged the world is terrible. That it has penetrated high places in the church is unthinkable. Yet such is the case.

To give just one example, the late Pope John Paul I praised Giuseppe Carducci, an Italian university professor, as an example of a good teacher of youth.[2] Who is the man recommended by no less than the Pope? Carducci became famous through his "Hymn to Satan," which begins: "My ardent verse is for Thee. I invoke you, Satan, king of the feast." It ends: "In holiness, incense and vows should ascend to thee, Satan. You have defeated Jehovah, the god of the priests."[3]

(I grant to this Pope that he might not have known whom he recommended, but it is wrong for a bishop to endorse an unknown.)

In 1949, a Soviet general said to a Catholic priest, Werenfried van Straaten, "We are Satan's elite, but you, are you God's elite?"

We must not remain silent about these matters.

We have seen in this book what length devil-worshipers are willing to go. May their dedication to evil be an incentive for us to behave like God's elite!

During the troubles in Poland in 1982, one could see mocking inscriptions on the walls. For example, "Marx said, Proletarians of the world, forgive me!" instead of the usual "Proletarians of the world, unite!"

I shuddered when I read these words.

Some have claimed about Engels that he repented before his death. There is no such record about Marx. In 1983, many commemorated the centenary of his death. Might he have held this same commemoration in hell?

While writing this book, I have passed many a sleepless night, thinking of what Marx must endure viewing perhaps in hell the rivers of tears and blood that he has caused to flow.

Jesus told a story about a rich man in the eternal fire who expressed one ardent desire: his brethren should be warned not to end up in the same place of torment (Luke 16:27,28).

Does Marx also have the same desire—that his followers should be warned not to walk in his footsteps leading to perdition?

Are the Polish people right when they have Marx say "forgive me"? Does he indeed cry out from the fire—as it might truly be—"Send someone to my house, for I have many comrades, so that he may warn them, lest they also come into this place of torment"?

The Soviet Communists did damage to their cause by disowning Stalin, who had become a popular idol. One can only speculate why they permitted such a reversal of policy, since it was certainly not in their best interests to remove Stalin's corpse from the mausoleum. Likewise, the Chinese Communists harmed their own cause by disowning Mao and jailing his wife.

Perhaps in the hidden depths of their souls, Soviet and Chinese Communist leaders felt what is now the burning desire of their former idols, who too late were remorseful about what they had done and taught.

As for me, I love every man, including Marxists and Satanists. If Marx and Engels and Moses Hess were alive today, my most ardent wish would be to bring them to Jesus Christ, who alone has the answer to man's ills and the remedy for his sins.

This is my wish for you, the reader. You have walked with me through the terrible pages of this book. Now I urge you to consider carefully your loyalties before it is too late. Abandon Satan and his evil cohorts. History proves he is never true to his own. Therefore, choose life and love and hope and heaven.

Marxists and proletarians of the world, unite around Jesus Christ!

CAN COMMUNISM BE CHRISTIAN?

Marxist "Christian" Theology

Ernesto Cardenal is a Catholic priest who is a self-avowed Communist and was active in the Communist government of Nicaragua. He is also one of the most prominent exponents of a theology that seeks to blend Christianity with communism.

Here are a few excerpts from his book *The Zero Hour:*

> A world of perfect Communism is the kingdom of God on earth. They are the same thing for me.... Through the Gospel I have arrived at revolution; not through Karl Marx, but through Christ. The Gospel caused me to become a Marxist.... I have the calling of a poet and prophet....
>
> Castro told me that the qualities of a good revolutionist are also the qualities of a good priest.... Let us not forget that the first Christians

were the best Christians, i.e., revolutionary and subversive Christians....

Marxism is the fruit of Christianity; without Christianity, Marxism would be impossible; Marx would be unthinkable without the prophets of the Old Testament. Changing the system of production, we can create the new man of the Gospel....

The Mexican Jesuit Jose Miranda says in his book *Marx and the Bible* that the Ten Commandments are Marxist, even the first commandment, to love God. For him, to love Jehovah above all means to love justice.... If the church ever asserted anything else, it was a monstrosity.

I believe that the Communists, too, belong to the church. I believe the true church includes many who don't perceive themselves as Christians, even those who consider themselves atheists. Many of these belong more to the church than some who sit in the Roman Curia.

Since Constantine, the church has always gone to bed with the state. If Christians and Marxists would read each other's writings, there would be no conflicts any more between Christians and Socialism.... It seems to me that worker-priests and revolutionists—the most progressive part of the church—are inspired directly by the Holy Ghost.

> For me the God of the Bible is also the
> God of Marxism-Leninism…. The apostle John
> says, "No one has seen God." What the atheist
> Marxists say is very much akin to what Saint John
> says: "No one has seen God."[1]

Another writer quotes Cardenal as follows:

> I am above all a revolutionist and as such fight
> for a Socialist country which is in the course
> of passing through a dictatorship of the prole-
> tariat, in which surely it cannot show itself feeble
> toward the enemies of its fatherland, not even in
> moments when one comes to the point of having
> to execute men for this purpose.[2]

It is self-evident that a man who thinks like this has no trouble praising the regime in Cuba as a model of liberty.

This errant belief is not an isolated phenomenon.

It is the by-product of an attempt to synthesize Marxism and Christianity; it is also seen in various forms of compromise in politics, art, economics, and so on.

Two Jews, Bernstein and Schwartz, composed the musical *The Mass* for the inauguration of the John F. Kennedy Center for the Performing Arts in Washington, DC, in 1971. In it, during the singing of the Kyrie Eleison, the Gloria, and the Credo, a band of singers and dancers howl their doubts:

God made us the boss;

God gave us the cross.

We turned it into a sword

To spread the word of the Lord.

We use his holy decrees

To do whatever we please. Yeah.

Give us peace that we don't keep on breaking.

Give us something or we'll just start taking.

We're fed up with your heavenly silence,

And we only get action with violence.

The "Christian" multimillionaires present at the concert cheered. Their wives, appareled in slit skirts and décolleté bodices, bejeweled and befurred, joined in the applause. The music is now standard repertoire.

I can understand men like the priest Cardenal. There is a ring of truth in the feeling he expresses of solidarity with the Communists, who appear to him as champions of the cause of the poor—always near to the heart of Christians.

In the Bible Job is called a righteous man. He describes to his dubious friends the program of his life:

> "I delivered the poor who cried for help, and the fatherless who had none to help him.... I was a father to the needy, and I searched out the cause of him whom I did not know. I broke the fangs of the unrighteous and made him drop his prey from his teeth." (Job 29:12,16,17)

These words could be uttered by any revolutionist.
Job continues:

> "Did not I weep for him whose day was hard?
> Was not my soul grieved for the needy?" (30:25)

> "If I have rejected the cause of my manservant or
> my maidservant, when they brought a complaint
> against me, what then shall I do when God rises
> up?" (31:13,14)

True believers have always reacted like this.

Cardenal's assertion that "the church has always gone to bed with the state" is untrue. For example, the war of secession in the United States, which led to the abolition of slavery, was influenced by *Uncle Tom's Cabin*, written by a Christian lady, Harriet Beecher Stowe. She said simply, "The Lord wrote it."

During a Communion service she had a vision of an old slave being beaten to death by a white ruffian. This became the story of Uncle Tom's flogging. The book was a stick of dynamite driven into the foundations of slavery.

Charles Spurgeon, the greatest Baptist preacher of the nineteenth century, was also an ardent fighter against slavery. He wrote, "I believe slavery to be a crime of crimes, a soul-destroying sin, and an iniquity which cries aloud for vengeance." William Wilberforce, a Christian and a capitalist, caused slavery to be abolished in the British Empire long before America's Civil War. Lincoln, also a Christian, issued the Emancipation Proclamation that freed the slaves in the United States. He stated, "If slavery is not wrong, nothing is wrong,"

These facts are widely ignored, especially in the Third World. Its theoreticians can call themselves Christian only because of the chaos in thinking prevalent in the church at this moment.

According to the July 28, 1949, decree of the Holy Office of the Roman Catholic Church, the following categories of Catholics are to be excommunicated:

> Whosoever belongs to the Communist Party;
> Whosoever makes propaganda for it in any way;
> Whosoever votes for it and its candidates;
> Whosoever writes for the Communist press,
>   reads and spreads it;
> Whosoever remains a member in a Communist
>   organization;
> Whosoever confesses the materialistic and anti-
>   Christian teaching of atheist Communism;
> Whosoever defends and spreads it.
> This punishment applies also to parties that
>   make common cause with Communism.

Many of the revolutionist theologians belong only formally to the Catholic Church, and yet have a great influence among believers. In the Orthodox churches, too, there exists a tendency to exploit, for the benefit of communism, the spiritual energies that religion awakens and channels.

These theologians proclaim an earthly paradise—communism, with capitalism as its foe. The church no longer waits for the coming of Jesus in the clouds of heaven. The triumph of communism will be equated with His coming. This explains why in Communist countries the God-hating Communist government has paid the clergy.

It needs to be said that among both Catholics and Orthodox, there are also bishops who fear absorption into earthly pursuits and seek rather a deeper spiritual life. Not all have bowed to Baal.

As for Protestants, in hearings before the US House Committee on Un-American Activities on February 26, 1966, Richard Arens, general counsel to the Committee, declared:

> Thus far, in the leadership of the National Council of Churches, we have found over 100 persons in leadership capacity with either Communist-front records or records of services in Communist causes. The aggregate affiliations of the leadership is in the thousands.

And the World Council of Churches for years has subsidized Communist guerrillas in Africa.

The Catholic Gustavo Gutierrez wrote, "The church must place itself squarely within the process of revolution."[3] The Lutheran theologian Dorothee Sölle, founder of Christians for Socialism, stated, "We are at the beginning of a new chapter in Christian history. It will not be written without Karl Marx."

These are the facts, open and uncontested, about what is happening in the church universal.

We did not heed the warning of the Lord to beware of wolves in sheep's clothing (Matthew 7:15). If the wolf speaks to us about doing good to mankind, we get hooked, forgetting that the worst of men can speak beautiful things.

German Socialists in 1907 opened their convention with Luther's hymn, "A Mighty Fortress," replacing "God" with "Socialist League." Some revolutionist groups practiced baptism. One called for a new Communion service at which the pastor would proclaim, "This is the body of the bread which the rich owe to the poor." Revolutionist groups spoke of "the holy Communist church," "the egalitarian church outside of which there is no salvation." Their "Communist Lord's Prayer" said, "No masters and no servants! Amen! Money and property shall be abolished!"[4]

The devil disguises himself as an angel of light. When the Communists came to power, unprecedented slaughters followed, which eclipse even Hitler's Holocaust.

Clergymen who had been on the side of communism also became its victims. If communism would conquer the countries of the Third World, these errant clergymen would sit in jail together with those who opposed this ideology.

Perfect Communism: Kingdom of God on Earth?

Cardenal says, "Communism and the kingdom of God are the same thing for me."

The word "communism" in itself is vague. It is taken to mean only an economic system in which everyone will work according to his abilities and will receive according to his needs. There will be no state, no division of the world into countries, and no social classes, because the means of production will belong to all mankind.

Suppose this could be attained—where is God in the picture? Why should this be equated with the kingdom of God? A society of unbelievers, even of men who hate and scorn God, could choose or be forced to live in such a state.

Scripture says that when the kingdom is the Lord's, "all the ends of the earth shall remember and turn to the LORD, and all the families of the nations shall worship before you" (Psalm 22:27).

The kingdom of God will not be a stateless society. The people of the saints of the Most High will have dominion over it (Daniel 7:27).

It is not a kingdom brought about by a political party, but by Jesus, the Son of Man (Matthew 16:28).

Obviously, there will be none of the evils that plague society now, such as war, famine, pestilence, pollution, injustice, exploitation, racism, etc. The kingdom of God will be one of righteousness, peace, love, joy, and the right to possess one's own mansion and garden (John 14:2).

Father Cardenal, who claims that he is a prophet, must know what his biblical predecessor Micah said: "In the latter days... they shall sit every man under *his* vine and under *his* fig tree" (4:1,4, emphasis added). The prophet Isaiah reinforces this idea: "They shall not build and another inhabit; they shall not plant and another eat" (65:22). Thus, Scripture endorses the notion of private ownership.

What would perfect communism look like in reality? Perfection as we humans experience it is the ultimate achievement of years of practice—in the field of sports, music, typing, or skills of any sort. A violinist perfects his performance of a Beethoven concerto by practicing his violin. A baseball pitcher achieves success by refining his technique through intensive, persistent effort.

Perfect communism, described as economic liberation, freedom, peace, and justice, could be attained only through the practice of such policies in the society it hopes to benefit.

But in actual experience Communists have jailed, tortured, and terrorized hundreds of millions of people for decades. How could such practice result in a just, mild, and loving society?

Christian communism is a utopian impossibility, a nightmare of exploitation. The theology of revolution is a patent absurdity, a contradiction in terms.

> What partnership has righteousness with lawlessness? Or what fellowship has light with darkness? What accord has Christ with Belial? Or what portion does a believer share with an unbeliever? (2 Corinthians 6:14,15)

"You cannot serve God *and* money," said Jesus (Matthew 6:24, emphasis added). Choose you this day whom you will serve.

NOTES

Editor's Note: When Richard Wurmbrand wrote this book, it was intended for the general population as a means to warn the reader "of the spiritual danger part and parcel of communism" (see p. xi). Selectively citing from the writings of Marx as well as others pertinent to his thesis, Richard Wurmbrand left the evidence with readers "to consider, weigh, and judge the documentation" for themselves. Such evidence includes periodicals, books, and other published works in a number of languages—including German, Russian, and French—which Richard Wurmbrand had collected, read, translated, and cited in this book. (Richard Wurmbrand frequently consumed content in a number of languages.)

Abbreviations used in these notes include:

MEGA: Marx, Karl and Engels, Friedrich, *Historisch-kritisch Gesamtaus-gabe. Werke, Schriften, Briefe* (*Complete Historical Critical Edition. Works, Writings, Letters*), on behalf of the Marx-Engels Institute, Moscow, published by David Rjazanov (Frankfurt-am-Main: Marx-Engels Archiv, 1927).

MEW: Marx, Karl and Engels, Friedrich. *Werke*. (*Works*)
(Berlin: Dietz-Verlag, 1974). The volume number
is in Roman numerals, the page number in Arabic
numerals.

CW: Marx, Karl and Engels, Friedrich. *Collected Works*
(New York: International Publishers, 1974).

Foreword

1. *Christ to the Communist World*, May 1969, p. 4.
2. Karl Marx and Friedrich Engels, *The Communist Manifesto*, in
Marx/Engels Selected Works, Vol. 1 (Moscow: Progress Publishers,
1969), p. 14.
3. Ibid., p. 34.
4. Stéphane Courtois, et al., *The Black Book of Communism: Crimes,
Terror, Repression* (Cambridge, MA: Harvard University Press,
1999), p. 4.
5. Marx and Engels, *The Communist Manifesto*, p. 34.
6. Richard Wurmbrand, *The Voice of the Martyrs*, February 1978, p. 4.

Chapter 1: Changed Loyalties

1. Karl Marx and Friedrich Engels, *Zur Kritik der Hegelschen
Rechtsphilosophie (Critique of the Hegelian Philosophy of Law)*,
MEGA, Introduction I, i (1), pp. 607, 608.
2. Rev. Paul Oestreicher, *Sermons from Great St. Mary's* (London:
Fontana, 1968), pp. 278–280.
3. Karl Marx, *Die Vereinigung der Gläubigen mit Christo* (*The Union of
the Faithful with Christ*), MEW, Supplement, I, p. 600.
4. Karl Marx, *Betrachtung eines Junglings bie der Wahl eines Berufes
(Considerations of a Young Man on Choosing His Career)*, ibid.,
p. 594. See also Robert Payne, *Marx* (New York: Simon &
Schuster, 1968), p. 34.

5. Karl Marx, *Archiv für die Geschichte des Sozialismus und der Arbeiterbewegung (Archives for the History of Socialism and the Workers' Movement)*, MEGA, I, i (2), pp. 182, 183.

6. Karl Marx, "Des Verzweiflenden Gebet" ("Invocation of One in Despair"), ibid., p. 30.

7. Ibid., pp. 30, 31.

8. Quoted in *Deutsche Tagespost*, West Germany, December 31, 1982.

9. Mikhail Bakunin, *Works*, Vol. III (Berlin, 1924), p. 306.

10. Karl Marx, "Spielmann" ("The Player"), *Deutsche Tagespost*, pp. 57, 58.

11. Anton LaVey, *The Satanic Bible* (New York: Avon Books, 1969), p. 29.

12. Anton LaVey, *The Satanic Rituals: Companion to The Satanic Bible* (New York: Avon Books, 1972), pp. 49, 50.

13. Karl Marx, *Oulanem*, Act 1, Scene 1, ibid., p. 60.

14. Ibid., Act 1, Scene 2, p. 63.

15. Ibid., Act 1, Scene 3, p. 68.

16. Karl Marx, *The Eighteenth Brumaire of Louis Bonaparte*, MEW, VIII, p. 119.

17. MEW, I, p. 344; I, p. 380; XXVII, p. 190; VI, p. 234.

18. Quoted in B. Brecht, *Works*, Vol. I (Frankfurt, 1979), p. 651.

19. Marx, *Oulanem*, Act 1, Scene 3.

20. Ibid.

21. MEW, XXX, p. 359.

22. Paul Goma, *Piteshti*.

Chapter 2: Against All Gods

1. Karl Marx, letter of November 10, 1837, to his father, MEW, XXX, p. 218.

2. Ibid., Heinrich Marx, letter of February 10, 1838, to Karl Marx, p. 229.

3. Ibid., Heinrich Marx, letter of March 2, 1837, to Karl Marx, p. 203.

4. Ibid., Karl Marx, "On Hegel," pp. 41, 42.

5. Quoted in *Deutsche Tagespost*, West Germany, December 31, 1982.

6. Karl Marx, "Das Bleiche Mädchen" ("The Pale Maiden"), MEW, XXX, pp. 55–57.

7. Müllern-Schönhausen, *The Solution of the Riddle, Adolf Hitler.*

8. Karl Marx, *Über die Differenz der Demokritischen und Epikureischen Naturphilosophie Vorrede (The Difference Between Democritus' and Epicurus' Philosophy of Nature)*, MEW, III, Foreword, p. 10.

9. Jenny von Westphalen, *Mohr und General, Erinnerungen an Marx und Engels (The Moor and the General, Remembrances about Marx and Engels)* (Berlin: Dietz-Verlag, 1964), pp. 273, 274.

10. Robert Payne, *Marx* (New York: Simon & Schuster, 1968), p. 317.

11. Ibid.

12. Karl Marx, *Die Rheinische Zeitung (Rhine Newspaper)*, "Der Kommunismus und die Augsburger Allgemeine Zeitung" ("Communism and the Augsburger Allgemeine Newspaper"), MEGA, I, i (1), p. 263.

13. Moses Hess, letter of September 2, 1841, to Berthold Auerbach, MEGA, I, i (2), p. 261.

14. Ibid., Georg Jung, letter of October 18, 1841, to Arnold Ruge, pp. 261, 262.

15. Marx and Engels, *Critique of the Hegelian Philosophy of Law*, p. 614.

16. MEW, I, p. 372.

17. Ibid., p. 386.

18. Hans Enzensberger, *Gespräche mit Marx und Engels (Conversations with Marx and Engels)* (Frankfurt-am-Main: Insel Verlag, 1973), p. 17.

19. James Hastings, *Encyclopaedia of Religion and Ethics*, Vol. XI (New York: Charles Scribner's Sons, 1921), p. 756.

20. Mikhail Bakunin, *God and the State* (New York: Dover Publications, 1970), p. 112.

21. Roman Gul, *Dzerjinskii*, published by the author in Russian (Paris, 1936), p. 81.

22. Enzensberger, *Conversations with Marx and Engels*, p. 407.

23. Pierre-Joseph Proudhon, *Philosophie de la Misère (The Philosophy of Misery)* (Paris: Union Générale d'Editions, 1964), pp. 199, 200.

24. Ibid., pp. 200, 201.

25. Paul Garus, *History of the Devil* (East Brunswick, NJ: Bell Publishing Co.), p. 435.

26. Heinrich Heine, *Works*, Vol. I, p. lviv.

27. Charles Boyer, *The Philosophy of Communism* (10: "The Political Atheism of Communism" by Igino Giordani) (New York: Fordham University Press, 1952), p. 134.

28. Marx, "The Player," pp. 57, 58.

29. Jerry Rubin, *Do It* (New York: Simon & Schuster, 1970), p. 249.

30. Karl Marx, "Menschenstolz" ("Human Pride"), MEGA, I, i (2), p. 50.

31. Ibid., Karl Marx, letter of November 10, 1837, to his father, p. 219.

32. Ibid., Georg Jung, letter of October 18, 1841, to Arnold Ruge, pp. 261, 262.

33. Arnold Künzli, *Karl Marx: Eine Psychographie (Karl Marx: A Psychogram)* (Zürich: Europa Verlag, 1966).

34. David Rjazanov, *Karl Marx: Man, Thinker and Revolutionist (Karl Marx: als Denker, Mensch und Revolutionär)* (New York: International Publishers, 1927).

35. Rolv Heuer, *Genie und Reichtum (Genius and Riches)* (Vienna: Bertelsmann Sachbuchverlag, 1971), pp. 167, 168.

36. Karl Marx, letter of February 27, 1852, to Friedrich Engels, MEW, XXVIII, p. 30.

37. Ibid., Friedrich Engels, letter of March 2, 1852, to Karl Marx, p. 33.

38. Ibid., Karl Marx, letter of March 8, 1855, to Friedrich Engels, p. 438.

39. Karl Marx, letter of December 2, 1863, to Friedrich Engels, MEW, XXX, p. 376.

Chapter 3: Ruined Faith

1. Franz Mehring, *Karl Marx—Geschichte seines Lebens (Karl Marx—Story of His Life)* (Berlin: Dietz-Verlag, 1964), pp. 99, 100.

2. Ibid., p. 97.

3. Ibid., p. 100.

4. Bruno Bauer, letter of December 6, 1841, to Arnold Ruge, MEGA, I, 1 (2), p. 263.

5. A. Melskii, *Evangelist Nenavisti (The Evangelist of Hate, Life of Karl Marx)* (Berlin: Za Pravdu Publishing House, 1933, in Russian), p. 48.

6. Friedrich Engels, *Dialektik der Natur (Dialectics of Nature)*, MEW, Introduction, XX, p. 312.

7. Friedrich Engels, poem probably written in early 1837, MEGA, I, ii, p. 465.

8. Ibid., Friedrich Engels, letter of July 1839 to the Graber brothers, p. 531.

9. Friedrich Engels, *Schelling, Philosopher in Christ*, CW, Volume 2, p. 191 (Berlin, 1842).

10. Ibid.

11. Friedrich Engels, *Schelling und die Offenbarung (Schelling and Revelation)*, MEGA, pp. 247–249.

12. Karl Marx and Friedrich Engels, *Selected Works* (London: Lawrence and Wishart, 1958), p. 52.

13. Ossip Flechtheim, *The Communist Party of Germany in the Weimar Republic* (Offenbach, 1948).

14. Künzli, *Karl Marx: A Psychogram*, p. 187.

15. Bertram Wolfe, *Marxism—One Hundred Years in the Life of a Doctrine* (New York: The Dial Press, 1965), p. 32.

16. Karl Marx and Friedrich Engels, *The Russian Menace to Europe* (Glencoe: The Free Press, 1952), p. 63.

17. Quoted in Wolfe, *Marxism*.

18. Friedrich Engels, MEW, VI, p. 176.

19. *Deutschland Magazine*, February 1985.

20. Quoted by Nathaniel Weyl, *Karl Marx: Racist* (New Rochelle, NY: Arlington House, 1979).

21. Karl Marx, MEW, XXXV, p. 122.

22. Chushichi Tsuzuki, *The Life of Eleanor Marx* (Oxford: Clarendon Press, 1967), p. 85.

23. Frederick Tatford, *The Prince of Darkness* (Eastbourne, UK: Bible and Advent Testimony Movement, 1967).

Chapter 4: Too Late

1. Sergius Martin Riis, *Karl Marx, Master of Fraud* (New York: Robert Speller, 1962), p. 11.

2. Edgar Marx, letter of March 31, 1854, to Karl Marx, MEW, II, p. 18.

3. Jenny Marx, letter (dated after August 11, 1844) to Karl Marx, MEW, Suppl. Vol. I, p. 652.

4. Franz Mehring, *Karl Marx—The Story of His Life* (New York: Covici, Friede, 1935), p. 18.

5. Ibid., p. 32.

6. Karl Marx, letter of May 20, 1882, to Friedrich Engels, MEW, XXXV, p. 65.

7. Walter Kaufmann, *Hegel* (Garden City: Doubleday, 1965), p. 288.

8. V. Illitch Lenin, *Complete Works* (Moscow: Political Literature Publishing House, 1964, in Russian), Vol. 48, pp. 226, 227.

9. Ibid., Vol. 45, p. 86.

10. Ibid., Vol. 54, pp. 86, 87.

11. "Budilnik," *Russia*, No. 48, 1883. Quoted in *The New Review*, New York: 140/1980, p. 276.

Chapter 5: A Cruel Counterfeit

1. George Katkov, *The Trial of Bukharin* (London: B. T. Batsford, Ltd., 1969), 1, p. 29.

2. Roy Medvedev, *Let History Judge* (New York: Alfred Knopf, 1971), p. 183.

3. F. J. Raddatz, *Karl Marx: A Political Biography* (Hamburg: Hoffmann und Campe, 1975), p. 32.

4. Boris Souvarine, *Stalin: A Critical Survey of Bolshevism* (NY: Longmans, Green & Co., 1939).

5. MEW, XXVII, p. 292.

6. Milovan Djilas, *Strange Times*, "Kontinent," 33, p. 25.

7. Ibid.

8. Svetlana Alliluyeva, *Twenty Letters to a Friend* (London: Hutchinson, 1967), pp. 64ff.

9. Ibid.

10. George Paloczi-Horvath, *Stalin* (Germany: Bertelmannsverlag, 1968).

11. Abdurakhman Avtorkhanov, *Criminals in Bolshevism* (Frankfurt-am-Main: Possev Verlag, in Russian), Grani No. 89–90, pp. 324, 325.

12. Abdurakhman Avtorkhanov, *The Provenience of Partocracy* (Frankfurt-am-Main: Possev Verlag, 1973, in Russian), pp. 198–201.

13. *Express*, Paris, October 6, 1979.

14. *Tempo*, Italy, November 1, 1979.

15. Peter Underwood, *The Vampire's Bedside Companion* (London: Leslie Frewin, 1975).

16. H. Knaust, *The Testament of Evil.*

17. Manfred Zach, *Mao Tse-tung* (Esslingen: Bechtle Verlag, 1969), p. 13.

18. MEW, V, p. 457.

19. Ibid., XXXI, p. 191; XXV, p. 179.

20. Ibid., VI, p. 283; VI, p. 286; VI, p. 279.

21. Lenin, *Collected Works*, Vol. 32, p. 281.

22. Aleksandr I. Solzhenitsyn, *The Gulag Archipelago* (New York: Harper & Row, 1973), Vol. I–II, p. 173.

23. *Russkaia Misl (Russian Thought)*, Paris, March 13, 1975, in Russian.

24. Rev. Dr. I. Nahyewsky, "Spomyny Polovoho Dykhovnyka," *America*, October 7, 1982, Vol. LXXI, No. 176, pp. 4, 18.

25. V. Ilyich Lenin, *Military Correspondence* (Moscow, 1954), p. 148.

26. Leon Trotsky, *Stalin*, quoted in *Novii Journal*, 158, p. 85.

27. Pierre Daix, *Picasso: The Man and His Work* (Paris, Somogy), p. 8.

28. Ibid., pp. 188–190.

29. Aleister Crowley, *The Book of Thoth* (Berkeley: Koshmarin Press, 1944), p. 97.

30. Ibid., pp. 134, 135.

31. Ibid., p. 137.

32. *Sovietskaia Molodioj (Soviet Youth)*, Moscow, February 14, 1976, in Russian, "Let Thy Kingdom Be Destroyed," p. 4.

33. *Rhein-Neckar Zeitung (Rhine-Neckar Newspaper)*, Heidelberg, February 5, 1968, "Kultusminister antwortet Studentenpfarrer" ("Minister of Cults Answers Youth Pastor").

34. *Paris-Match*, December 10, 1982.

Chapter 6: A Spiritual Warfare

1. *Kommunisma Uzvara (Victory of Communism)*, Riga, April 1974, in Lithuanian.

2. Anatolij Levitin-Krasnov, *Böse Jahre (Evil Years)* (Lucerne: Rex-Verlag, 1977), pp. 144, 145.

3. *Pravoslavnaia Rus (Orthodox Russia)*, San Francisco, No. 20, 1977, in Russian, "Satanist Worshippers," pp. 9–12.

4. D. Bacu, *Piteshti* (Madrid: Colectia Dacoromania, 1963, in Romanian), pp. 71, 187.

5. *Cuvantul Romanesc*, Canada, February 1980.

6. Hermann Hartfeld, *Irina* (Chappaqua, NY: Christian Herald Books, 1981).

7. Karl Marx, *Theories of Surplus Value*, MEW, XXX, p. 375.

8. A. Reghelson, *The Tragedy of the Russian Church*.

9. *Catacombes*, France, September 1980.

10. Salu Ndebele, *Guerrilla for Christ* (Old Tappan, NJ: Fleming H. Revell), pp. 9, 10.

11. *Impact*, Switzerland, February 1981.

12. "Chronicle of the Lithuanian Catholic Church," No. 44, 1981.

13. Priest Dudko, *O Nashem Upovanti (About Our Hope)* (Paris: YMCA Press, 1975, in Russian), p. 51.

14. Igor Shafarevitch, *La Legislation sur la Religion en URSS (Religious Legislation in the USSR)* (Paris: Seuil, 1974, in French), pp. 67–71.

15. Sheila Ostrander and Lynn Schroder, *Psychic Discoveries Behind the Iron Curtain* (Englewood Cliffs, NJ: Prentice Hall, 1970).

16. *Novie Russkoie Slovo (New Russian Language)*, New York, July 30, 1975, in Russian, "Para-Psychology in the USSR," p. 2.

17. MEW, II, p. 9.

18. Bakunin, *Works*, Vol. III, p. 206.

19. Quoted in Arnold Künzli, *Karl Marx: A Psychogram*, p. 403.

20. MEW, XXVII, p. 107.

21. Ibid., p. 351.

22. Konrad Low, *Why Communism Fascinates* (Germany: Deutscher Institute Verlag, 1983).

23. *Christian News*, March 4, 1985.

Chapter 7: Marx, Darwin, and Revolution

1. H. Montgomery Hyde, *Stalin: The History of a Dictator* (London: Rupert Hart-Davis, 1971), pp. 28, 29.

2. Gregory Fremont-Barnes, *Encyclopedia of the Age of Political Revolutions and New Ideologies, 1760–1815* (Greenwood Press, 2007), p. 329.

3. Karl Markus Michel, *Politische Katechismen: Volney, Kleist, Hess (Political Doctrines: Volney, Kleist, Hess)* (Frankfurt-am-Main: Insel Verlag, 1966); Moses Hess, *Red Catechism for the German People*, pp. 71–73.

4. Hess, letter of September 2, 1841, to Berthold Auerbach, MEGA, I, i (2), p. 261.

5. Jung, letter of October 18, 1841, to Arnold Ruge, ibid.

6. Moses Hess, *Rome and Jerusalem* (New York: Philosophical Library, 1958), p. 10.

7. Ibid., p. 15.

8. Moses Hess, *Ausgewählte Schriften (Selected Works), Rome and Jerusalem* (Cologne: Melzer-Verlag, 1962), p. 229.

9. Ibid., p. 18.

10. Ibid., p. 27.

11. Ibid., pp. 236, 237.

12. Ibid., p. 308.

13. Ibid., p. 243.

14. Ibid., p. 324.

15. *Kommunistisches Bekenntnis in Fragen und Antworten (Communist Credo in Questions and Answers)*, ibid., p. 190.

16. *Die Eine und Ganze Freiheit (The One and Only Total Freedom)*, ibid., p. 149.

17. *Philosophie der Tat (The Philosophy of Action)*, ibid., p. 138.

18. Karl Marx, "On Hegel," MEW, XXX, pp. 41, 42.

19. Edmund Silberner, *Moses Hess* (Leiden: Brill, 1966), p. 31.

20. Ibid., p. 32.

21. Ibid., p. 121.

22. Ibid., p. 421.

23. Dudko, *About Our Hope*, p. 53.

24. Silberner, *Moses Hess*, p. 421.

25. Ibid.

26. Ibid., p. 418.

27. Moses Hess, *Philosophische Sozialistische Schriften, 13, Über das Geldwesen (Philosophical Socialist Writings. About the Monetary System)* (Berlin: Akademie-Verlag, 1961), p. 345.

28. Hess, *Selected Works, Rome and Jerusalem*, p. 44.

29. Ibid., p. 10.

30. Moses Hess, *Briefwechsel (Correspondence)*, letter of December 9, 1863, to Lassalle (The Hague: Mouton & Co., 1959), p. 459.

31. Karl Marx, *Das Kapital (The Capital)*, MEX, XXIII, p. 779.

32. G. W. F. Hegel, *Werke. Fragment über Volksreligion und Christentum (Works. Fragment on Popular Religious Beliefs and Christianity)* (Frankfurt-am-Main: Suhrkamp Verlag, 1971), I, pp. 35, 36.

33. U. Steklov, *M. A. Bakunin, His Life and Activity* (Moscow: Literature Publishing House, 1937), Vol. 3, p. 435.

34. Quoted from *The Catechism of the Revolutionist* by Dostoyevski in his *Complete Works*, Vol. 12, p. 194.

35. Ibid., *The Demons*, Vol. 10, p. 312.

36. Ibid., p. 322.

37. Ibid.

38. Ibid., p. 324.

39. A. I. Volodin, Y. F. Karjakin, and E. G. Plymak, *Tchernishevsky or Netchaiev* (Moscow: Koriakin and Pleeman, 1976), p. 247.

40. V. Burtsev, *During 100 Years: Compendium of the History of Political and Social Movements in Russia* (London, 1897), p. 94.

41. Volodin et al., *Tchernishevsky or Netchaiev*, p. 223.

42. E. S. Vilenskaia, *Revolutionist Underground in Russia* (Moscow, 1965), p. 398.

43. Volodin et al., *Tchernishevsky or Netchaiev*, p. 223.

44. Ibid., p. 155.

Chapter 8: Angels of Light

1. Anton LaVey, *The Satanic Bible* (New York: Avon Books, 1969), p. 29.

2. Ibid.

3. Ibid., pp. 30, 31.

4. Anton LaVey, *The Satanic Rituals: Companion to The Satanic Bible* (New York: Avon Books, 1972), p. 1.

5. Ibid., pp. 38–53.

6. *Selections from Nietzsche* (New York: Viking, 1954), p. 600.

7. *Yuni Kommunist*, Moscow, December 1984.

8. David Rjazanov, *Karl Marx: als Denker, Mensch und Revolutionär (Karl Marx: Man, Thinker and Revolutionist)* (Vienna: Verlag für Literatur und Politik, 1928), pp. 149, 150.

9. Künzli, *Karl Marx: A Psychogram*, p. 352.

10. Moshe Glickson, *The Jewish Complex of Karl Marx* (New York: Herzl Press, Pamphlet No. 20, 1961), p. 40.

11. Künzli, *Karl Marx: A Psychogram*, p. 361.

12. Ibid., pp. 323, 373.

13. Karl Marx, letter of January 16, 1861, to Lassalle, MEW, XXX, p. 578.

14. Robert Payne, *Marx* (New York: Simon & Schuster, 1968), p. 306.

15. William Tyndale, *Works* (Parker So., 1849), quoted by the *Oxford English Dictionary* (Oxford: Clarendon Press, 1933), Vol. VIII, p. 735.

16. William Shakespeare, *Complete Works* (Glenview: Scott, Foresman, 1973), *Midsummer Night's Dream*, Act II, Scene I, 33–34, p. 189.

17. Alexei Stjusev, "An Unforgettable Night," *Svenska Dagbladet (Swedish Daily News)*, Stockholm, January 17, 1948, in Swedish.

Chapter 9: Whom Will We Serve?

1. Solzhenitsyn, *The Gulag Archipelago*, Vol. III–IV, p. 10.

2. *Nauka I Religia (Science and Religion)*, Moscow, December 1976, in Russian, Vol. 12, pp. 73–76.

Chapter 10: Marx or Christ?

1. *Idea*, June 3, 1983.
2. *Osservatore Romano*, September 17, 1978.
3. Quoted in Gerhard Zacharias, *Satanskult und Schwarze Messe (The Cult of Satan and the Black Mass)* (Germany: Limes verlag, 1964).

Appendix: Can Communism Be Christian?

1. Ernesto Cardenal, "The Zero Hour," *Zero Hour and Other Documentary Poems*, Donald D. Walsh, ed. (New Directions, 1980).
2. INF of *Aide á l'Église en Détresse*, April–June 1980.
3. Gustavo Gutierrez, *A Theology of Liberation* (Maryknoll, NY: OrbisBooks, 1973), p. 135.
4. James Billington, *Fire in the Minds of Men* (New York: Basic Books, 1980).

ABOUT THE VOICE
OF THE MARTYRS

The Voice of the Martyrs (VOM) is a nonprofit, interdenominational Christian missions organization dedicated to serving our persecuted family worldwide through practical and spiritual assistance and leading other members of the body of Christ into fellowship with them. VOM was founded in 1967 by Pastor Richard Wurmbrand and his wife, Sabina. He was imprisoned fourteen years in Communist Romania for his faith in Christ, and Sabina was imprisoned for three years. In 1965, Richard and his family were ransomed out of Romania and established a global network of missions dedicated to assisting persecuted Christians.

To be inspired by the courageous faith of our persecuted brothers and sisters in Christ advancing the gospel in hostile areas and restricted nations, receive a free subscription to VOM's award-winning monthly magazine. Visit us at vom.org or call 800-747-0085.

To learn more about VOM's work, please contact us:

United States	vom.org
Australia	vom.com.au
Belgium	hvk-aem.be
Canada	vomcanada.com
Czech Republic	hlas-mucedniku.cz
Finland	marttyyrienaani.fi
Germany	verfolgte-christen.org
The Netherlands	sdok.org
New Zealand	vom.org.nz
Singapore	gosheninternational.org
South Africa	persecutionsa.org
South Korea	vomkorea.kr
United Kingdom	releaseinternational.org